MarriageBiz

By Stephanie Weiland Knarr, Ph.D.
With Brendan Dean Knarr

KNARR PUBLISHING, LLC

Dedication

To Brendan Knarr, my devoted husband.

To my alma mater, Creighton University, whose teaching of "Service to Others" has influenced my professional work.

About The Author

DR. STEPHANIE WEILAND KNARR is the owner of Stephanie Weiland LLC, a popular marriage and family therapy practice in Metropolitan Washington D.C. Raised on a Nebraska farm, she brings the down to earth family values and work ethic from America's Midwest to her family therapy business. Dr. Stephanie has been a licensed clinical marriage and family therapist in Maryland since 2002. She is an Approved Supervisor and Clinical Member of the American Association for Marriage and Family Therapy.

Currently, Dr. Stephanie Weiland Knarr lives with husband Brendan Knarr in Laurel, MD. They are co-directing their family organization and raising three children: Rachel, Luke, and Gavin. Dr. Stephanie is a professional speaker and the creator of AmBizious Families programs and seminars.

You can contact Dr. Stephanie Weiland Knarr through her website at www.marriagebizonline.com.

Acknowledgements

I have many people to acknowledge and thank for *servicing* me during the writing of MarriageBiz. I am thankful to my number one, Mr. Brendan Knarr, for encouraging me. I think my marriage to Brendan is a great example of MarriageBiz and for that I am truly blessed. Brendan was instrumental by incorporating some of his ideas and points of view regarding both personal and business relationships to the MarriageBiz concept. When it came to contributing, editing, formatting and revisions, Brendan was truly my helpmate! Finally, he took the lead on setting up Knarr Publishing, LLC and the publishing of MarriageBiz.

I would also like to acknowledge four professional colleagues who reviewed MarriageBiz. Dr. Carol Werlinich, Licensed Clinical Marriage and Family Therapist and professor at the University of Maryland Marriage and Family Therapy program reviewed the book, gave me encouragement, and shared constructive feedback for improvement. Merlene Blair-Brown, Licensed Clinical Marriage and Family Therapist of Owings Mills, MD also reviewed MarriageBiz and encouraged me. While completing research for

Marriage Biz, I happily discovered that Dr. John Curtis, author of <u>The Business of Love</u>, has some similar ideas about using business concepts to create more successful marriages. He graciously agreed to review and support MarriageBiz. Finally, Djarta Halliday completed some of the research for MarriageBiz and inserted some of the footnotes. She also reviewed a first draft of the book and shared some constructive feedback to improve it.

I also must acknowledge my many loyal clients who have learned from my MarriageBiz metaphors. At times, couples commented that the metaphors and examples from MarriageBiz helped them better communicate with each other. I have learned many things from my couples who willingly share their hearts and make themselves vulnerable. It is an honor to learn about the ups and downs of marriage from such wonderful people.

I am very appreciative of my graphic designer for the book cover, my sister-in-law Jennifer Weiland. She really took to heart what I was looking for – a modern, simple cover for MarriageBiz. Also, I am thankful to my brother, Carl Weiland, for agreeing to attend and video my book-signing and kick-off MarriageBiz seminar. Credit also goes to our professional photographer,

Lauren Fitzgerald Photography of Howard County, Maryland. Thanks to Lauren, who provided a great photo of Brendan and myself for our first book venture. I am also grateful to Stephen Hudak, owner of Black Cat Press, for advising Brendan regarding the ins and outs of publishing. Finally, a shout out to Robert Gatewood of the Marketing Pulpit and Stubbs of Leap of Faith for promoting MarriageBiz on their radio shows.

Most importantly, although I am respectful of the many diverse beliefs of my clients and acquaintances, I cannot give thanks without acknowledging my own relationship with Christ who called me to serve married couples. Only God truly knows my deepest heart and all of my unique struggles to write MarriageBiz. So, to God, I am thankful for helping me to hold onto the light of Christ.

Dr. Stephanie Weiland Knarr

Table of Contents

Introduction

A business cannot succeed without providing prompt and skilled customer service that resolves complaints. Without customer service to fix the mistakes that humans inevitably make, trust and security are lost - customers will eventually choose to conduct business elsewhere. Likewise, a marriage cannot succeed without two people, both with an attitude of prompt and caring service for their significant other's complaints. Research on marriage communication has found that one of the primary causes of America's high divorce rate is that the 'customer service departments' of our marriages are failing miserably!

Well, I think it is time we change that... MarriageBiz is meant to inspire the attitude of service towards our marriages that we already have in our business and military cultures. Worldwide, America has a leading business economy and a great military. Now, MarriageBiz utilizes an innovative approach to help couples transfer the service-oriented attitude and skills they already have in their business and civic life right into their marriage relationships. With an American attitude of service applied to our marriages, I have no doubt that the MarriageBiz program will help create far more happily ever-afters.

Chapter 1

To Love, Honor, AND SERVE

Imagine yourself walking up to the relationship service counter. You are very satisfied with your marriage most of the time, but right now you have a complaint that you want addressed! There is a big sign and it flashes "RELATIONSHIP SERVICE." The sign is at the front of your house *and* below there is another sign that tells you what hours the department is open. You are pleased to see that the Relationship Service Department is open several times a week during times that are convenient for your schedule. When you go to the relationship service counter, your sweetie does a good job servicing your complaints. As a result, you feel confident and secure about your romantic relationship. You also feel that your spouse values you and your marriage contract.[1]

MarriageBiz is a straightforward book meant to inspire an American attitude of SERVICE in our

---

[1] Wives make the majority of complaints in marriage. Recent thought suggests that one of the reasons for this is that today's couples are seeking greater equity in the marriage contract according to Professor David Smith of Ohio State University (1998).

marriage relationships.[2] In a nutshell, this book takes a business model of customer service skills and applies it to marriage relationships. Hence, the title is "MarriageBiz." This book is short because I hope that it can be helpful to many people, possibly even to those many husbands who are not inclined to read long self-help books!

Marriage Biz is based upon solid experience and research. I have been conducting marriage therapy for over a decade after completing both a Master's Degree and a Ph.D. in marriage and family therapy. I have been running my own business since 2002, and I was raised by parents who are small business owners. I am also the wife of a business man.

My husband, Brendan Knarr, has also influenced the writing of MarriageBiz. He claims that this is a "well-balanced book" because it includes the husband and business man's perspective! Brendan (my sweetie) has been involved in business for nearly twenty years with various job descriptions. He obtained a Bachelor of Science degree studying business and government

---

[2] MarriageBiz principles and steps can also be used to increase the success of other romantic relationships (for example, in dating relationships, while preparing for marriage, or in committed romantic partnerships).

with a minor in psychology from Shippensburg University of Pennsylvania. Brendan is currently a successful sales manager for a large steel company. Along with his contributions to this book, both on a personal and business level, Brendan edited and managed the publishing of MarriageBiz.

There are many good *reasons* for you and your significant other to learn MarriageBiz skills.

Reason #1. The skilled servicing of business complaints leads to profit and success. However, skilled customer service is a learnable skill that does not come naturally to most people. People who are skilled in business customer service have had training that helps them learn how to not withdraw or attack when customers are making complaints.

Brendan has said that in his sales and customer service training he has been taught that the number one priority in good business service is listening to the customer. Too often, a customer service representative mistakenly talks about themselves or what they think instead of listening carefully to what is important to their customer.

A business that is primarily profit-oriented often does not thrive long-term. The solely profit-oriented business is generally a less healthy environment for both employees and customers. Likewise, in a marriage, if one partner is primarily motivated by money that is not enough. Business relationships and romantic relationships both thrive when there is an atmosphere of providing service, listening and resolving complaints, and showing interest in the overall wellness of other people.

Reason #2. Marriage research shows that the skilled servicing of marriage complaints is one of the primary predictors for marriage success.

Dr. John Gottman found in his reputable research on married couples[3] that one of the major predictors for divorce is the following: Husbands are failing to "be influenced" by their wives complaints and concerns. Also, wives are not using "slow start up"

---

[3] Drs. John M. and Julie S. Gottman are the leading experts on marital communication. Together they founded and direct the Gottman Institute and the Relationship Research Institute in Seattle, Washington. For more information, visit: http://www.gottman.com.

when they communicate complaints to their husbands.[4] The United States has one of the highest divorce rates in the world.[5] What this tells me is that the customer service counters of American marriages are failing!

Reason #3. There are many people who are successful in their business and work life who are failing in their personal relationships. In these cases, husbands and wives are not transferring good business skills into their marriage communication. If you are successful in your work life but have had failed or troubled romantic relationships, then MarriageBiz is for you!

---

[4] Research by Dr. Gottman has found that wives bring more complaints to the marriage relationship and that husbands are not being influenced by their wives complaints. However, my observation is that both husbands and wives will benefit from improving how they service their spouse's complaints. Furthermore, one cannot overgeneralize. In some relationships, I have observed that the husband brings up more complaints to his wife.

[5] The United States has the highest divorce rate compared to other countries according to numerous references, for example: http://www.nationmaster.com/graph/peo_div_rat-people-divorce-rate.

During my work with couples in the past ten years, I have become more and more intrigued about this fact:

Many men who are effectively able to respond to customer complaints in their business, professional, and work life struggle to do so effectively in their romantic life with their wife or girlfriend. Many women who are effectively able to get complaints resolved in their consumer life struggle to do so in their romantic life with their husband or boyfriend.

So, I decided that if I can help men and women transfer and use the same skills from their business and consumer life into their personal life, then relationship problems can get resolved more effectively![6]

Another author, Dr. John Curtis wrote <u>The Business of Love</u> (Curtis, 2006). He also encourages couples to apply business concepts to their romantic relationship. However, Dr. Curtis is focused on assisting couples with creating a vision statement, writing

---

[6] While completing research for MarriageBiz book, I discovered another book, <u>The Business of Love,</u> which also encourages the application of business principles to the marriage relationship (Curtis, 2006).

objectives, outlining a budget, identifying job descriptions, and scheduling review meetings. The Business of Love has a different, broader focus than MarriageBiz. I highly recommend couples consider reading The Business of Love in addition to MarriageBiz.

During my training as a family systems therapist, I learned the solution-focused model of systems therapy. [7] This model encourages therapists to creatively help clients look at strengths and skills they already use in one part of their life and apply those skills to a different part of their life.

When I first started using MarriageBiz principles to help couples "service" each other's complaints, I was using this solution-focused marriage therapy approach. MarriageBiz ideas came to me one step at a time during my hours spent with couples who were learning to resolve conflict. I wanted to find examples that my clients could relate to, and many couples could relate easily to business and consumer examples. So, I began regularly teaching my clients to apply skills they already knew from their business and consumer life into their

---

[7] Family systems therapists are trained to think of family organizations as having similar organizational and systemic principles as other organizations and cultures – to include business organizations, cultural organizations, and government organizations.

marriage relationships. My clients were very receptive and responded well to the ideas, and thus MarriageBiz was created.

Reason # 4. MarriageBiz is a great review of business service principles and skills for corporate employees and small business people who want to improve or freshen-up their business service skills.

Customer service training is incredibly important in the business world. I have been a small business owner servicing complaints for ten years. In addition, I help families diffuse conflict and de-escalate emotions every day. I know business customer service and relationship service like the back of my hand. I think my MarriageBiz seminar is great training for corporations and small businesses because it teaches and refreshes customer service skills, but with a different spin on it! Marriage Biz seminars spice up customer service training with a family-friendly dimension. Marriage Biz is a win-win for family-friendly company trainings.

Reason #5. Even if your marriage relationship is satisfactory now, following the attitudes and steps in

MarriageBiz is a great way to prevent future relationship problems and maintain a happy marriage. From a personal standpoint this is not only a good personal relationship decision, learning how to prevent future problems via servicing of marriage complaints it is also a smart financial decision. Yes, sometimes people are often thinking of marriage entirely from a romantic or sexual perspective, they forget about the business end of things. Marriage is still a legal contract. Quite simply, it is a financially-sound business decision to maintain a happy marriage; reason being that divorce and the division of assets can be very costly to your financial future.

Hopefully, by presenting the information above, I have now persuaded you that relationship SERVICE is very important in marriage and romantic relationships. After all, one of the major predictors of divorce is that the customer service counters of American marriages are failing! In my mind, it makes no sense that American marriage service counters are failing. Why do I say this?

Americans *know* SERVICE.

You *know* SERVICE.

Here are some facts to support the fact that Americans already have a great attitude of service.

> ➤ America thrives on a SERVICE-oriented economy. Yes, America's economy is struggling right now. But we are still one of the most highly developed economies around the globe.
>
> ➤ America's military is a powerful force to be reckoned with. Yes, men and women protect our liberties and SERVE our country well.
>
> ➤ On the recent decade anniversary of 9/11, there was honor and appreciation shown for the SERVICE attitudes of our police and firefighters.
>
> ➤ The diverse religions that make up America all encourage an attitude of SERVICE. For example, Christian scripture narrates Jesus modeling humility and service when he washed the feet of his disciples at the Last Supper.

We owe it to our partners and our children to transfer our SERVICE attitudes and skills right into our marriages! What makes me even more excited about MarriageBiz is that families can role model for children the service skills that they will need in the adult business world. Therefore, the interchangeable skills of

MarriageBiz can be used to increase American success in business, community, *and* family life.

You might be thinking - what about people who have not had job training in customer service or business models? How will MarriageBiz help these individuals transfer business skills into their marriage? MarriageBiz also helps people transfer skills and communication that they see and hear literally every day as consumers. And we all know there are few Americans who are not good consumers!

I think Americans simply have a different attitude and response in our business, consumer, work, and military life than we do in our romantic, marriage, and family relationships. Most people have great intentions. After all, people who get married vow to love, honor, and care for one another. No one vows that they will love and honor their spouse except for when their spouse complains about them! Instead, we vow that we will love and honor our spouse all the time, *even when they complain.*

So, I am suggesting that we have our vows say, "I promise to love, honor, and SERVE you. Love and honor are often thought of as "feeling" words. The words love and honor are tied up with ribbons and bows and all kinds of romantic notions for most people. Make no mistake though, the word SERVE is undoubtedly an action word. As soon as you hear the word serve, don't you think about "doing, helping, fixing, protecting?"

Imagine if we used the word SERVE in our marriage vows? How many more marriages would be successful if we were to change our attitudes about SERVICING our partner's complaints! In Chapter 2 of MarriageBiz I will teach you the principles and attitudes you need for having an effective relationship service department.

I have found that many people who engage in marriage counseling[8] absolutely have an attitude of service in their work, religious, and civic life. These are the kind of people, for example, who tear up with thoughts of patriotic service to country when they hear the Star Spangled Banner. But somehow that attitude of service just doesn't translate when their spouse or girlfriend rings the bell at the relationship service desk - if you know what I mean.

---

[8] The case examples I refer to in MarriageBiz are not my real life clients. Names and identifying information have been changed to protect the privacy and confidentiality of married couples I have assisted. Rather, the case examples in MarriageBiz are generalizations of the presenting problems and treatment of many couples I have seen for marital therapy.

Granted, I understand that hearing the marriage customer service bell can be difficult. You are most vulnerable at home, in your marriage. It can be hard to hear your spouse complain about you. After all, you much prefer kissing, date nights, and making love. But, if you have not figured this out already, your spouse is going to complain about you. Sometimes your spouse will take your character flaws, whatever they might be, and try to steer you in a different direction.

So, really, if you want to have a significant other in your life, then you have a choice to make. Here are your choices. Are you going to create an effective and prompt service department for your relationship's concerns, making it more likely that your marriage will last? Or, are you going to wait until every last ounce of trust has been lost? If you choose not to recognize potential problems and resolve issues when your mate rings the service bell, the trust in the relationship slowly deteriorates. Sooner or later, your mate may give up all together.

When I say your mate will "give up," I think there is usually one of three devastating consequences:

> Even if your mate remains married to you, you will never know how happy your

marriage could have been, how romantic and delightful your wife would have been, if only you had shown her that she was a valuable and important person to you at the service counter.[9] In other words, your marriage is quite likely to be far less satisfying for both of you.

> Your husband or wife will walk away from your relationship possibly never trusting in romantic relationships again. He or she may rather live alone than to have the frustration of knocking at a partner's service door repeatedly only to find out that it is always closed - or to receive the message that he or she is not valued enough to have his or her complaints resolved.

> Your spouse will divorce you in pursuit of a new, trusting relationship with a partner who has a skilled relationship service department.

---

[9] The words husband/wife, he/she can be used interchangeably throughout MarriageBiz.

Let me close out this chapter by acknowledging that I understand something:

Listening to complaints from your spouse and resolving them will not be the most pleasurable part of your marriage.

Similarly, any small business owner will tell you that resolving complaints is not why they went into business! Most went into business to provide a service or product that they are good at and enjoy providing. Furthermore, they most likely went into business to make money.

People get married because they yearn for a helpmate, for companionship, for children, passion, and for greater financial security. No one ever says, "I know-- I'll get married so I can service my spouse's complaints!"

So, the point is that complaint resolution is not what people are thinking about when they start a business or a marriage. Servicing complaints will likely be one of the most difficult, least pleasurable parts of your job as a spouse. But, I am recommending that you become successful at this part of your marriage job description.

Having a relationship service department for your marriage that works properly is 100% necessary in order to keep the relationship you desire for all of the *other* reasons I just mentioned, such as: a helpmate, companionship, passion, children, and greater financial security.

Anyone who has ever had to be a customer service representative knows that it is far easier to handle complaints after being trained with the proper skills and tools. MarriageBiz can help you learn the skills you need and make it easier to resolve your mate's complaints. This is my mission. Now, let me teach you how to take the skills you already use in your business and consumer life and apply those to your love life. [10]

---

[10] Throughout the MarriageBiz program, I use business metaphors that will help you to improve your relationship success. However, I do recognize that marriage relationships have some differences from the typical consumer/business relationship. The romantic relationship is very dynamic. Both husband and wife have very diverse, sometimes competing desires and needs.

Chapter 2

Do You Have A Customer Service Department for Your Relationship?

Do you have a customer service counter for your mate? To answer this question, think about how you usually react when your husband or wife complains; especially if it is about something *you* did (or didn't do). Or think about how you react when they appear upset, angry, or moody. I have observed that quite often, people respond poorly to these kinds of situations. In fact, there are some people who completely ignore or dismiss their spouse's complaint. Certain behaviors basically tell your mate that you do not have a relationship service department.

Behaviors that say "I do not have a relationship service department" for your complaints:

➢ Shutting down and not saying anything.

➢ Rolling your eyes in the back of your head.

➢ Changing the topic to something else more pleasant.

➢ Shifting the topic to a complaint that you have about your spouse. (Sure, you can bring up complaints as well, but I recommend you start with resolving your partner's complaint first.)

> Strong arming your partner by dominating the conversation, taking all the air time, or talking over your partner.

If you do any of the above when your mate complains, I highly recommend that you learn new ways to react. Instead, I urge you to open up your relationship service department.

Ignoring, avoiding, or dismissing your wife or husband's complaint is similar to not having a customer service department. Imagine being a consumer with a problem. You walk into the place of business only to find out there is no customer service department. You can't believe it! There is no manager at this business who takes complaints; or there is, but he's never there. Each time you try to get your complaint resolved, you get more frustrated. How frustrated you are depends upon how much you need the product or service at that time.

Please, try to put yourself in your spouse's shoes. If your spouse keeps walking to the relationship service counter only to find there is no one behind it, he or she is likely to become more frustrated with each attempt.

Similarly, if you keep calling 1-800 NO ONE IS HOME to register your complaint and no one answers, your resentment and anger is likely to build up.

Now, let's assume that you do have a customer service department for your relationship. Even though you want to make your wife happy and try to fix the problems she has brought to you, somehow these conversations result in a fight! When this occurs, it could be similar to you walking up to a business service counter and being greeted by a representative that has not had the proper training. Since they do not use the right customer service skills, they actually say things that make you become even more frustrated or upset.

MarriageBiz is meant to teach you the right attitudes and skills to resolve complaints in your relationship. In this chapter, I will be teaching you service attitudes that will help you as a relationship service representative. I will teach you the specific steps that will help you resolve relationship service complaints in a later chapter.

MarriageBiz Service Attitude #1: Even if you are getting it right 95% of the time, it is normal for your spouse to complain about the other 5%.

Even if you are an excellent spouse in many ways, your husband or wife may sometimes still have complaints and ask you to make adjustments. In particular, the adjustments you are asked to make are often due to a personality weakness you have.

For Wives

If you are a woman, think of it this way. You frequent a small boutique that has great products. The owner is very good at creating a wonderful atmosphere and purchasing unique items for her customers. The staff is very pleasant and the boutique is in a great location. These are all characteristics of a great business. However, the owner has a weakness. She is so focused on the creative part of her business that she has failed to create a good system for handling returns and refunds. So, even though you like the boutique location, the atmosphere, and the products, you have made complaints about how her employees respond to returns. It may take many complaints and adjustments from numerous customers before the boutique owner gets her system improved.

Your marriage is the same way. Your husband is likely to ask you to improve parts of yourself that need more work. This does not mean that you are not being a great wife, or that you don't have many positive qualities. It just means you have some room for improvement.

For Husbands

Since I know you could not resist reading the caption above "for wives" you may already have gotten the point. If not, try thinking of it this way. Let's say you are an avid car collector and you regularly take your vehicles to be serviced, maintained, and repaired at a local mechanic's shop. The mechanic is an honest guy, and he has a reputation for telling the truth about what is wrong with your vehicles and how much it will reasonably cost to repair them. But the owner has a weakness. He is very sociable and good-natured. He has extended conversations with every customer who walks through the door. As a result, his shop is inefficient and it takes half the day to get your automobile serviced! Even though you like his store location, trustworthiness, and friendliness; you complain to the owner about how long you have to wait for the service. It may take many complaints and adjustments before he learns that his customers prefer efficiency over his friendliness!

On the other hand, your mechanic's competitor across town may not be as personable and is more expensive, but gets the job done more efficiently which frees up time in your schedule. This is appealing to you. Now, I am not telling you to run out and switch mechanics or spouses, but rather to register your complaints and also work on your own weaknesses.

You are not human if you don't have your character flaws. In fact, there is a good chance that you will be a better, more well-rounded person if you hear your partners concerns and make adjustments to improve your personal weaknesses.

A typical thing that can happen is your spouse complains about the way you do something. Suddenly, the switch goes off in your head that makes you think about all the times you did something right. Let's say that you forgot to pay your joint credit card bill on time one month. Your partner is upset about the fact that your mistake is putting a ding in both of your credit scores. You respond by saying, "Good grief. You are acting all crazy over one time that I forgot to do something?"

Let's look at what is wrong with this thinking: Imagine if a restaurant owner were to tell a customer,

"Good grief, the last 8 times you came to our restaurant we gave you perfect service and a great meal. Now the one time that we screwed up your order, you are going to complain? Are you crazy?!" Fortunately, this is not how most business owners and managers handle complaints. Rather they strive for a customer to be satisfied all the time. They know that customer satisfaction is not always going to exist, but it is their goal. If their company makes a mistake, normally the business person will listen, apologize, and make it up to their customer via a free product or some other incentive to maintain and rebuild the relationship.

In marriage, the fact of the matter is that even if you are getting things right 95% of the time, your spouse may still have a complaint when you make a mistake. This is normal. Sometimes, you may not hear enough appreciation for the 95% of the time you are doing things correctly. In this case, you can ask your partner for more appreciation by filing a complaint at their relationship service desk. However, it is still imperative that you service your partner's complaints.

MarriageBiz Service Attitude #2: If your spouse complains, consider it a good thing. It means she or he is still doing business with you. Be ready to service relationship complaints!

Okay, I realize that this is really turning lemons into lemonade! After all, it's pretty sour hearing your husband tell you he thinks that you are becoming a Facebook addict. Or, men, hearing your wife tell you that you are turning into a caveman. I've noticed most people do not like to hear their spouse complain about them, *especially in those instances when they know they are right!*

Here's the good news. If your spouse is still ringing the relationship service bell, it means you are in business! You are in a relationship with your mate. They still have a trusting relationship with you. They believe in you, like you, and think you are going to help resolve their concerns. And if you love your sweetie, then that is a very good problem to have - if only you have the skill set to then resolve their concerns. (And I know that part can be confusing, so I will be teaching you the steps for relationship service in Chapters 4 and 5).

Servicing a customer's complaint takes patience and the ability to really focus attention on the customer and the root cause of their complaint. If a business representative multitasks while resolving a customer complaint, they are less likely to have a positive outcome. When your spouse makes a complaint it is likewise very important to put down your cell phone, shut off the television, and put away anything else that might have you preoccupied. Or you can see if your spouse is willing to schedule a future time to discuss the matter when your relationship service counter is open and you are not preoccupied.

MarriageBiz Service Attitude #3: Being married does not mean you can stop doing good business.

Imagine that sales woman Jeanie courts a new account. During the courtship, she promises that her company has a great product and that she will provide good service. Eventually, her courting pays off, and she signs a contract with her new customer. Jeanie then still has to follow through on the promises she made to her customer during the courtship. Would it make sense for her to not keep her promise of providing a great product and service? Well, of course not. Eventually, that might lead to the loss of the customer relationship and potentially the entire account.

Similarly, after you get married, you have to keep servicing your spouse. Whatever you promised your spouse during your courtship needs to be delivered for years to come. If you do not keep your promises, eventually that could lead to the loss of your marriage relationship.

One good business practice in sales is to conduct regular "checking in" with customers. Proactively following-up in a customer-based relationship makes a customer feel valued.

Quite the opposite, some people make the mistake of becoming complacent in marriage instead of staying proactive. They start thinking they've "tied the knot" – the deal is already sealed. In this case, a husband or wife mistakenly assumes that their spouse will stay with them because of the marital promise, and they lose focus on what they promised to do.

Sadly, the above is sometimes a mistaken assumption. I cannot tell you the number of clients who I have seen in individual therapy right after their husband or wife has walked out the door and filed for divorce. Some of my clients state something to the effect, "I never thought my spouse would leave me." When I take time to break down the situation, I find that my client assumed their partner would honor the marriage commitment "till death do us part." But when I explore further, I often find out that my client who has just been "left" was not honoring their marriage contract to Love, Honor, and SERVE. He or she was almost always able to tell me numerous problems in the marriage that went unresolved. However, they were not thinking of their marriage in terms of a contractual relationship which needed servicing. In the end, their spouse ended up filing suit for divorce.

If you want to remain married, then I strongly urge you to stay focused on doing "good business" and satisfying your spouse. As I discussed in Chapter 1, "To love, honor, and care for means "To SERVE." In order to keep your marriage vows, you are required to have humility and to provide service to your spouses' complaints. In essence, you continue to court your spouse and provide good service so the relationship stays positive, trusting, and satisfying.

MarriageBiz Service Attitude #4: If you do not properly respond to relationship complaints, your wife or husband may not want to shop at your store as often.

Think about it. You shop at your favorite store regularly. You develop a relationship with the store manager. You stop by weekly to see what new products and window displays they have. Things are wonderful until one day you have a problem with one of the products you purchased. You approach the manager and state your complaint, hoping the product or problem will be fixed. The manager tells you that you are making too big of a deal of things and goes back to his little manager's office and drinks his coffee. Yikes!

The next time you have some shopping to do, you are hesitant to conduct business at your favorite store. However, you like the products, the location, and the people so much (except for one bad experience), that you decide to give the store another try. You say to yourself, "Maybe the manager was just having a bad day." You again have many good experiences until there is a problem again. You again go to the manager and state your complaint. Again, he tells you "tough luck," makes you look like a pouting child, and walks back to his little manager's office to sip his coffee.

At this point, you are so annoyed that you only go back to that store if you really need something – or only for specific products or services. In fact, if you can get some of the items you need from somewhere else, you do. You may only go back to that store if they have a product or service you can't find anywhere else, such as an imported wine or a collector's trinket.

The same is true with your love relationships. If you are like the manager who dismisses complaints, your spouse will not want to shop at your store as often. OK men, pay attention here - when the lights are low and the kids are in bed, you might just want your wife to shop at your store, if you know what I mean... Women, the same is true for you. When it is Sunday morning and you want your husband to take you and the kids on an outing to the shopping mall (he's not really into the mall scene), you want him to shop at your store, if you catch my drift.

People are typically having more sex and going to more shopping malls together during the early stages of their marriage. Whatever your mate did for you at the beginning of the relationship, they are more inclined to continue those same behaviors if you properly service their complaints. When you service complaints at the relationship service counter, you create a scenario where your mate wants to keep shopping at your store.

MarriageBiz Service Attitude #5: If you want to figure out what your partner thinks is a fair marriage contract, listen carefully when he or she complains.

Simply put, marriage requires ongoing contractual negotiations. Exactly what your spouse is looking for to have a fair marriage contract will come to light in their complaints. For example, imagine you are a gal who watched Monday night football during dating, engagement, and early marriage. But now you have a toddler in the house. Once the baby came, no more Monday night football for you! Your husband starts to complain one night that you won't sit down to watch NFL with him. Meanwhile, you have just finished putting up dinner and are settling down your toddler for bed. You are thinking to yourself, "Good lord, how can I watch Monday Night Football when I am putting Charlie to sleep? He is lucky that I take care of the house and family so *he* can watch football."

However, instead of saying this, you stop yourself from reacting. You open up your relationship service counter. You find out rather quickly that your husband understands that you can't watch Monday night football and put the baby to bed at the same time. The resolution he suggests is that he hire a babysitter twice during the season so you can snuggle on the couch one night with popcorn, and the other night go out to watch the game. It's a deal!

Whatever it is that your mate feels is important to the marriage contract will usually come out as a complaint. So, listening to your spouse's complaints and acting on them is extremely important to having a satisfactory marriage.

MarriageBiz Attitude #6: Prompt and reliable relationship service breeds security, trust, and communicates value. Poor relationship service breeds feelings of insecurity, mistrust, and devalues your partner.

I want you to think about yourself as a consumer with a complaint. When you make your complaint by calling up the business customer service phone number, you are either met with prompt and skilled service, or you are met with slow, unskilled service. When you are getting prompt and skilled service, you likely feel important, confident, and secure about your consumer/business relationship. When the service is slow and you are not responded to with proper assistance, you feel unimportant to that business. A loss of trust and a sense of insecurity encroach upon that consumer/business relationship.

For example, when you call ABC Company, you are met very quickly with a human who picks up the phone to find out exactly what you need. They are energetic and polite. As a result, you like ABC Company and you feel important. You have the sense that ABC Company is honest. In contrast, when you call XYZ company, you get the automated customer support line. They wear you out punching in numbers and waiting through various menus before you even get to state your complaint. Then, you either give up, or become so frustrated because of the process that when you do finally get the chance to speak with someone you come across as abrasive.

When it is finally your chance to speak, you are told that you will need to speak with a manager. Now you have to spend more time on hold. You lose trust that XYZ will ever service your complaint. You may even wonder if XYZ is cheating you with their prices because of the lack of service. You feel unimportant and uncertain about your future business dealings with XYZ.

A similar dynamic is true in marriage. The better you are at providing prompt, reliable, and helpful service, the more your wife or husband is going to feel important, valued, secure, and trusting. In most cases, this will also mean a happier spouse, less conflict, and more pleasant memories together. Isn't that what most of us strive for in our relationships?

On the other hand, if you are not consistent and do not provide skilled servicing of complaints, your spouse is likely to start feeling unimportant, insecure, and will sometimes even mistrust you. As a marriage therapist, I have seen many spouses feeling so devalued at the relationship service counter that they also begin to wonder if their spouse is having an affair. They have no evidence of their spouse betraying them with another man or woman; however, because they are being cheated and devalued at the service counter, they become suspicious about being cheated in other aspects as well.

Perhaps you have the intention of providing consistent service to your mate's concerns and complaints. However, ask your mate: "Do I resolve your complaints in our marriage?" If they say no, then read and digest the upcoming chapters. Your heart may be in the right place. You just need to learn proper relationship service skills and then get some practice using them!

Chapter 3

Making Your Complaint at the Relationship Service Counter

You are a valued consumer. You are also a valuable mate. This means that many of your concerns need to be resolved at the relationship service counter in order for you to have a happy, secure romantic relationship.

My recommendation is that you follow strategies and steps at the relationship service counter similar to how you act as a consumer at the customer service counter. [11] I have noticed that some people, who are skilled as a consumer, do not remember to use the same strategies when they are upset with their spouse. That is, the same woman who confidently asks for a resolution to her complaint at the customer service

---

[11] "Softened start-up" is a communication technique that encourages a reasonable, calm approach to making marriage complaints. "Softened start-up" is the ability to gently start talking about a complaint or problem with one's partner while avoiding criticism. This technique increases the likelihood that a woman's complaint will be resolved by her male counterpart (Gottman, Gottman, & DeClaire, 2006).

counter in a business establishment, such as a clothing store, is an emotional wreck when seeking resolution from her romantic partner. I realize that most of you do not relish the task of going to the customer service counter. However, hopefully you will agree with me that you are more likely to get what you want if you follow certain steps!

Imagine yourself at the customer service counter when you are having a good day. You are calm and reasonable. Now, think of one of those not so good days – you know, the kind when you have gone to the customer service counter after you've been stuck in traffic with your kids fighting with each other in the back seat. On these days, you are frustrated and irritated, as opposed to calm and reasonable. Now I'd like you to think about which frame of mind is most likely to lead to a positive resolution of your consumer complaint.

Naturally, when you are reasonable and follow certain thoughtful strategies, you are more likely to get your complaints resolved quickly and effectively. Now, let's walk through what these steps are and apply them to your marriage relationship.

MarriageBiz Complaint Step #1: Think about what would resolve your complaint before you make it. Spend some time considering the following: what end result would satisfy you?

Consumers are accustomed to thinking about what they want before they go to the customer service counter. For example, consumers want a new product to replace the defective one. Or, they want a refund because a product or service is not the quality they desired. In some cases, they want an apology. In other cases, they may want to know how the company will change their policies. Depending upon the circumstances, some consumers want a gift card, discount or free product to "make up" for some kind of inconvenience that the company caused them. Those free desserts restaurants hand out when they make mistakes are even tastier when they are free. As a consumer, you are accustomed to asking for and receiving some of the resolutions I just mentioned.

Well, I'd like you to start applying these same principles to your romantic and marriage relationships. However, in the personal arena of marriage it can be difficult if you are not accustomed to thinking in this way. I've noticed that in the complicated world of romantic relationships, people are less accustomed to considering what they would like as an end result.

It is a key relationship skill to identify your ideal resolution in advance of registering your complaint.

In many cases, people have had previous romantic or family relationships (such as a parent/child or a sibling relationship) where their complaints were ignored, minimized, or were met with anger or guilt trips. For these people, because of past history, they feel helpless to have their personal concerns resolved. In essence, a person with a history of not getting their complaints addressed at the "relationship service counter," may anticipate never getting their complaints addressed. Ultimately, they do not even think about the resolution they are looking for! Instead, because they anticipate not being valued at the relationship service counter, they build resentment and anger; and they feel very emotional and helpless. This usually means they are far away from identifying a resolution.

Let's look at another example. Mary's parents did not allow her to express herself while she was growing up. If she asked for something, she was sometimes told that she was selfish. She was taught to follow parental rules, complete her chores, and go to school. If she complained about anything, she received disapproval, a guilt trip, or in some cases a punishment.

Fast Forward. Now, Mary is married to Joe, and they have three young children. She is completely overwhelmed with the busy family life of young parents, but when she and Joe have a problem she does not complain. Her resentment grows until she is crying and upset – then her numerous complaints about Joe come spilling out. Mary has not given thought to what would resolve her complaints because she was taught as a child that she is not supposed to complain or request that someone listen to her concerns.

Joe looks at Mary as if she is a dramazilla. He quickly becomes frustrated because he feels that Mary is having an emotional meltdown "for no reason," and he does not know how to service her emotional complaints. Joe is anxious after a long day at work and has no idea what Mary wants him to do in order to fix the problems they are having. Joe just wants Mary to stop crying. If Mary were to ask Joe for what she needs, her wish would be his command. He wants his wife to be happy, but he does not know how to help make her happy when she starts crying.

The problem here is that Mary does not even know exactly what she wants to help her feel content, resolved, and peaceful! She has not identified in advance what she would ideally like for a resolution.

I have seen this problem frequently since becoming a relationship therapist. Quite often, a wife or husband has a complaint but a sense of helplessness sets in before they think of a resolution. Because of terrible past experiences at the relationship service counter, a wife assumes that her husband is not going to resolve her concern. So, she comes to the relationship service counter upset, emotional, and angry *without an identifiable resolution.*

If you think that you are a person who does not identify the resolution you want before you make a complaint, then it is really important that you concentrate on using this MarriageBiz step. Even if you have not had good experiences getting past concerns resolved at the relationship service counter; keep in mind that your current boyfriend, girlfriend, or spouse may be willing to give you exactly what you are asking for in order to resolve your complaint - if only you can spell it out to him or her. Give it a try by completing the following exercise:

Think of a current or recent problem that you have had in your relationship that was not resolved. What outcome would make you feel better? That is, what would solve the problem for you? What is it that you would like from your partner?

Here are some common examples of resolutions in romantic relationships for you to think about:

➤ Would you like an apology?
➤ Can you think of a new agreement you can ask your partner for that would prevent the same problem from happening in the future?
➤ Is there something you could ask your partner for that would help "make it up to you?"
➤ Would you simply like your spouse to listen and verbalize that they understand your feelings about something?
➤ Would you like your spouse to promise to discontinue a certain behavior? Or conduct a certain behavior more regularly?

Now, plan out what you will say to your partner. Practice asking for the resolution you are looking for. Give it a try, and it might actually make you feel more confident in expressing your concerns. As you are practicing this exercise, remember the following:

➢ You are important and valuable, and your concerns in your relationships ought to be resolved in some way.

➢ The love in your life might just be the kind of person who is generous and who services complaints. Just because you had poor relationship service in the past does not mean you will always receive poor relationship service in the future. In fact, I recommend that you invest in relationships with people who give good relationship service.

➢ If you are in a relationship with someone who does not resolve your complaints, try following the MarriageBiz Complaint Steps. Doing so may improve your success at getting complaints resolved. If not, you might consider requesting that your spouse read MarriageBiz Chapters 4 and 5.

MarriageBiz Complaint Step #2: Start by saying something positive about your romantic relationship and your mate. A customer who starts out by calmly stating, "I really like doing business here because I love your products, however I am having a problem" is more likely to get their complaint resolved.

Likewise, it is a great idea to start out by telling your husband that you appreciate that he is a great provider before complaining that you don't like how he leaves his empty soda bottles in the vehicle. By starting out with a positive, you are increasing the chances of getting the solution you are looking for.

People like servicing someone that respects and appreciates them.

The fact of the matter is that most people like servicing someone who they feel likes and appreciates them. If you skip this step, then you are not setting the right stage for having your complaint serviced. By expressing what you appreciate about the relationship, you are reminding your partner that you like them, respect them, and that you appreciate your relationship with them. This approach increases the likelihood that they will listen and resolve your complaint. By starting with MarriageBiz Complaint Step #2 you are also promoting yourself as a reasonable, respectful person.

MarriageBiz Complaint Step #3: Tell your mate that you are giving them the benefit of the doubt. For example, you can communicate that you know they did not intentionally create this problem. *Notice that you are now on step 3 and you have not yet stated your complaint!* You are continuing to set the stage for appearing reasonable and calm. This is absolutely necessary for getting your complaint resolved. If you forget this step, there is a good chance that your partner is going to start explaining that they did not intend to make a mistake, frustrate you, or create a problem. Then the conversation becomes focused on intention rather than upon resolution.

In a business context, a consumer might say something to the representative like, "I know you didn't create this problem," or "I know that your company did not realize that this product was defective when you sold it to me, but ...." Or, another example is to say, "I am really angry right now, and I don't want to take this out on you. But you need to be aware that your company is failing at providing quality service and I need to register my complaint."

In your romantic relationships, you will increase the likelihood of your complaint being resolved if you start out by giving your spouse the benefit of the doubt. You can do this by mentioning "I understand that you were not intentionally creating a problem." It is important that you quickly remove this potential roadblock so that you can get straight to discussing the resolution you want. Here are some examples of things you can say to give your spouse the benefit of the doubt:

➤ "Honey, I know you don't like to upset me and you probably did not mean to hurt my feelings, but the fact is that you did."

➤ "You are a very good husband to me, so I know that you did not mean to create a problem, but I have a concern I'd like to speak address with you."

➤ "I know you love me and would do anything for me. So I'm trusting that you will be able to help me with this problem I'm having."

MarriageBiz Complaint Step #4: *Briefly* state only one complaint in two to three sentences. Laundry lists get dirty and convolute the real message you want to communicate. So, notice I emphasize "briefly" state your complaint. This is especially true for the women. Most women (including myself) are not short on words, but truly one of the places in your life that you will benefit from being less descriptive is when you are complaining about what you don't like about your partner's ways. If you want a successful marriage, spend less time describing why things bother you. Instead, direct your emotional and mental energy into following all of these strategies and steps!

Look, I understand that sometimes you are going to have a bad day. The kind of day where your preschooler kept you up with an earache, you were late to work because you forgot to put gas in the car the night before, and your cell phone was going off repeatedly during an important meeting. When you have a bad day, it is quite likely that you will be so frustrated that the MarriageBiz Complaint Steps will go right out the window! You may forget to follow the steps that will help your relationship complaints get resolved. When this happens, I hope your spouse will improve their relationship service response by following the MarriageBiz steps to servicing your complaint outlined in Chapters 4 and 5.

However, on your good days, your relationship will benefit if you are able to save the details when you are complaining. If possible, try not to elaborate on the numerous ways that your husband's inconsiderate behavior caused you a scheduling nightmare. He may get lost in the details and lose sight of the root cause of your complaint. That is why it is important to keep your complaint very, very brief. *In fact, try to say your complaint in two or three sentences. Then STOP!!!*

MarriageBiz Complaint Step #5: Tell your spouse that you have a resolution in mind that you'd like to request. In this step you are continuing to be reasonable and calm. You are letting your spouse know that you have thought about this situation - and that there is something they can do to help fix the problem. People generally like to fix problems and help their mates, so it is good if you can spell out what it is that you would like them to do.

Now, ask for the proposed resolution that you thought of back in step #1. If you are open to other possible resolutions, tell your spouse that you will consider other possible ideas as well.

Hopefully, you are confident and able to ask for what you would like as a possible resolution, because you thought about it ahead of time and you believe that you are making a reasonable request! Remember that you are valuable and important. Also remember that you need to have your complaints serviced to maintain a happy, healthy romantic and marital relationship!

MarriageBiz Complaint Step #6: Finally, when your spouse agrees to a resolution that you feel good about, say thank you and accept the resolution.

For example, if your mate apologizes, try saying, "I accept your apology." Too often people will continue to express their feelings and thoughts after they've already gotten an apology or received a resolution they've asked for.

There are times when I have observed people worrying or doubting themselves, "Did I ask for too much?" For example, there are times when I have observed women saying, "Maybe I'm being too hard on him." The same women then feel guilt-ridden and do not graciously accept the resolution that their spouse has just agreed to. These same women would be far less guilt-ridden if the restaurant who messed up their order gave them a free dinner. Nor would these women be concerned about the profit margins of the store that gave them a refund for a defective product.

If you are a partner who has a hard time saying thank you and accepting when your spouse does something nice to fix your relationship concerns, then you are a part of your marriage problem. You are forgetting that you are valuable and important in your marriage, just as you are in your consumer/business relationships. You bring certain qualities and strengths to the marriage partnership.

When your husband or wife listens to you and agrees to give you the resolution you asked for - take it and run with it! If you have a husband who will service and resolve some, if not most of your complaints, then count your lucky stars and enjoy your life! Instead of being guilt-ridden, try telling him how much you appreciate that he takes your relationship seriously enough to resolve your concerns. You can tell him that reaching resolution regarding your concern helps you to trust him even more!

Asking for Comfort from Your Mate

One of the things that people often joke about is that men like to fix problems while their wives, on the other hand, just want to share their *feelings*. Women, when you are sharing feelings with him, he is likely to perceive that you are complaining – even if you are not complaining about him! Therefore, I recommend that you run through MarriageBiz Complaint Steps when you want to share your feelings or ask for comfort from your spouse.

For example, maybe you are upset and want to complain to your husband about a disagreement you had with a friend. You believe that if you can talk and he listens to you for about 5-10 minutes that you will feel better (You have identified a resolution which is MarriageBiz Step 1). This complaint is not about your husband, so it seems like you wouldn't need to follow steps 2 and 3. But if you can start out by telling him he is great (MarriageBiz Complaint Step 2) and that you want to share your feelings, and that you have a complaint but is not at all about him (MarriageBiz Complaint Step 3), then you are setting the stage to have him listen and preventing him from drifting in to defense mode.

Next, follow MarriageBiz Complaint Step 4 and explain briefly, in less than 2 sentences, that you had a disagreement with your friend. Tell your husband that he can help resolve the concern you are having if he will listen to you for about five to ten minutes without giving you any advice (MarriageBiz Complaint Step 5).

Now, you've just outlined how your husband can help resolve your *feelings*. He believes his role is to make you happy. In about 20 – 30 seconds he knows why you are emotional, that the complaint is not about him (whew!), and that his listening to you for 5- 10 minutes will help you feel better. This works great. Your husband gets to fix the problem by listening to you, and you get to share your feelings. He just needs to understand that the way he can fix the problem *is* by listening to your feelings so that he knows exactly what his role is in the discussion.

Have you ever noticed that sometimes you start expressing emotions to your spouse and you are seeking comfort but somehow it turns into a fight? Using the MarriageBiz complaint steps can help when you are emotional, upset, or needing comfort.

When you are seeking comfort from your spouse, instead of bursting into tears or starting to rant about your boss, try to start out by calmly asking for comfort via MarriageBiz Complaint steps.

When you want comfort from your mate, try to spell out exactly what kind of comfort service resolution you want. For example, I suggested above that you might ask him to listen to you for a few minutes until you feel better. But sometimes you may want a different kind of comfort. For example, you may like it when he holds your hand. It is important that you learn what comforts you and then follow the complaint steps above to ask for comfort.

If your spouse does not typically comfort you, then think about how you would like him to comfort you. Then, you can ask your spouse for the type of comfort response you would like the next time you are upset. What would make you feel better?

Here are some possible resolutions you can ask for when you are seeking comfort from your mate:

- To hug you or to hold you while you are falling asleep.
- To run the bath water for you.
- To get you a glass of water or something to eat.
- To go on a short walk with you.
- To watch television with you, read to you from a book, or play a game of cards with you.
- To rub your back or hold your hand.

For many people, it is hard to ask for comfort. However, taking this step to ask for resolution in the form of asking for comfort when you are moody, upset, or sad will help your spouse know what they can do to protect and care for you. Otherwise, if you are upset, emotional, or complaining and do not tell your spouse how they can comfort you, then this may cause them to feel helpless. Helplessness breeds frustration and fighting! So . . . asking for the comfort you need from your partner could ultimately prevent an escalation which leads to fighting.

Chapter 4

MarriageBiz Steps for Skilled Relationship Service

Your marriage cannot be completely trusting, secure, and successful without a skilled "relationship service department." Your relationship service department should be constantly listening for the bell to ring at the service department counter. You will know the bell is ringing when:

> ➤ Your spouse is upset, crying, angry, irritable, or moody and quiet.
>
> ➤ Your spouse makes a complaint about your behavior (e.g., something you did or didn't do).
>
> ➤ Your spouse complains about your character flaws or personality differences.
>
> ➤ Your spouse complains about other things unrelated to the marriage. For example, they complain about someone else's behaviors or character flaws. (In this case, they are not asking you to service a complaint about your marriage. They are more likely looking for you to service them in the way of providing comfort, understanding, or advice).

How would you grade the "relationship service department" for your marriage? More importantly, what grade would your mate give you? To give yourself a grade, answer the following Yes or No questions.

Y   N   When your spouse is upset, do you start out by saying, "You are important to me, and I don't like to see you so upset."?

Y   N   When your spouse is complaining (about your behavior or about something else), do you listen without interrupting?

Y   N   Do you regularly ask your mate, "What can I do to resolve this for you?" or "What can I do to comfort you?"

Y   N   Do you ask your husband or wife if you have made them feel better or if you have fully resolved their concern?

Y   N   When your spouse is upset, do you engage in reflective listening, such as saying, "So, your concern is _____? Is that right?"

There is not a magic answer key to these questions. The answers are not buried deep in my book nor will you have to turn the book upside down to read the answers to these questions. Simply, if you answered Yes to all five of these questions, then you have an A in relationship service skills. If you answered No to at least some of these questions, then you are likely missing some important steps that will help you have a more successful, secure marriage. In order to teach you steps for resolving your spouse's concerns, I will be walking you through the steps that a business representative uses to resolve complaints.[12] Then I will discuss how you can use these same steps in your relationship to effectively resolve problems.

MarriageBiz Step 1: Tell your spouse that you value them and that you don't like seeing them upset. If your spouse is upset with you, apologize and ask for forgiveness.

First, let's take a minute to think about how a properly trained customer service person starts out addressing a complaint. For example, customer Bob phones the customer service department at XYZ Appliances. Maria, who has been well-trained at servicing customer complaints, answers the phone. Bob

---

[12] I have crafted MarriageBiz Service Steps from Inghilleri and Solomon's (2010) book Exceptional Service, Exceptional Profit: The Secrets of Building a Five-Star Customer Service Organization.

then angrily complains that the new dishwasher he just purchased last month is already broken. (He is angry because his wife and his crying infant are stressing him out. They have little time to wash the dishes by hand because they have a new baby in the house). Fortunately, Maria knows how important it is for her to take the first proper steps when a customer is upset or angry: diffusing the customer's negative emotions. She says, "Bob, you are a valued customer here, and we don't like seeing you dissatisfied. I sincerely apologize that you are going through this inconvenience today." [13]

Bob is surprised at Maria's response. He was half-expecting XYZ Appliances to drag their feet. In fact, he anticipated that he would probably get an automated response and that they wouldn't even have someone picking up the phone! When Maria picks up the phone and energetically tells him that he is a valued customer, his anger goes from a 10 down to a 4. He is glad to know that XYZ values him, and he feels that they are heading in the direction of resolving his concern.

---

[13] Inghilleri and Solomon recommend business representatives who service customer complaints start out with a sincere apology, diffuse emotions, and build an alliance with the customer.

On the other hand, let's imagine that Maria is not properly trained at servicing customer complaints. When Bob calls up (with his baby screaming in the background) and makes his angry complaint, Maria says, "I don't know why you are ranting at me. I didn't break your dishwasher. It's not my fault you are stressed out from having a new baby. Don't have sex if you can't handle having children."

Now, Bob really has steam coming out of his ears and is ready to blow a gasket. He then proceeds to make other complaints and things escalate. Bob explains to Maria that XYZ Appliances could not fix his old dishwasher and sold him a new one. Then XYZ Appliances took a month longer than promised to install the new dishwasher - which was a huge inconvenience. Now, the new dishwasher, that he dipped into his savings to purchase, is broken and he is doubly angry because he was promised this dishwasher would be AMAZING for his busy young family.

Maria then says, "I'm not sure if we will be able to help you fix this, we'll have to send out a repair person – the cost will be $100 for the service call and we can provide service between 8 and 12 or between 1 and 5." Now, Bob is even angrier because the repair will cost money and he will have to take off work. Bob is fit to be tied over how inconvenient purchasing a product from this XYZ Appliances has turned out to be! You can see the path this situation is taking, and it is not a smooth one!

Likewise, I have noticed that most conflicted couples fail to complete MarriageBiz Step #1. As a result, they end up on a very bumpy road in the beginning and conflict starts to escalate.

Unfortunately, the types of comments I observe spouses making to each other on my couch are similarly not leading down a smooth path. For example, I observe them saying comments such as:

- "I am sorry you feel that way."
- "I think you are overreacting. I did not mean to do that."
- "Why are you yelling at me? I didn't do anything."
- "You are expecting me to get things perfect all the time. You are too critical."
- "I am working so hard. I just can't believe that you think I'm not doing enough!"

I believe it is unfortunate that people naturally respond this way, because most of my clients have great intentions. They absolutely want to have a happy marriage, but they are not properly trained on how to create a secure relationship when it comes to resolving the complaints of their loved ones. Even a well-meaning, attentive spouse often moves straight to MarriageBiz Steps 3 or 4. However, because their spouse's angry emotions are not diffused; Steps 3 or 4 do not work.

Completing MarriageBiz Step 1 sets the tone for a caring, service-oriented discussion. You are basically telling your mate that you love and honor them, that you want them to be happy and pleased, and that you desire to make things better. You have set the stage for properly resolving your spouse's complaint.

I definitely recommend that you think of a thoughtful way to tell your mate that you value them. Here are some examples of ways to diffuse your mate's emotions by telling them that you value them:

➤ "You are my number one. I hate seeing you upset, and I want to fix this problem so that you feel better."
➤ Quietly say, "I do not like seeing you upset sweetie. You mean a lot to me."
➤ "Honey, you are important to me, and I want to work this out with you."

> "You are a really good wife and mother. I want to resolve this so that you are happy."

Whatever you do, you must role play and practice how you plan to communicate with your wife or husband the fact that you value them. Why, you ask? Because, taking this step is an extremely important step in the right direction. If you skip over this step or you don't do it well, then you are putting yourself at greater risk for an altercation. Assuming that you don't like altercations, then I encourage you to make expressing value to your spouse as second nature as checking your investment portfolio, planning your grocery list, or brushing your teeth. This is a MUST DO! It is important to plan how you are going to communicate with your sweetie that you value them when they have a complaint.

MarriageBiz Step 2: Listen without interrupting while your spouse elaborates about their complaint.[14]

---

[14] Inghilleri and Solomon suggest that the second step is to go over the complaint with the customer. MarriageBiz Steps 2 and 3 are basically meant to assist you in going over your spouse's complaint. Listen carefully.

Now, I am going to go back to customer Bob and well-trained customer representative Maria. After diffusing Bob's emotions, she says pleasantly to Bob "Now, why don't you start by telling me more about what has been going on with your dishwasher." After an effective customer service person diffuses negative emotions by expressing they value their customer, the next step is to say "Will you tell me more about the problem that you are having?" Then, the customer service representative listens patiently and does not interrupt. Sometimes, the representative may even allow the customer to complain and express various frustrations for several minutes.

If your spouse is mad at you, after you've diffused conflict, I urge you to offer to listen to the problem. [15] For example, you can say:

➢ Will you tell me all the reasons that you are mad at me so I can understand?
➢ Please tell me more about the things that are bothering you.

---

[15] This positive action is an example of what is called "turning toward." It involves showing that you are open, willing to listen, and primed for a discussion about the problem (Gottman, Gottman, & DeClaire, 2006).

> I will listen to your feelings about what I did to upset you so that you can get this off your chest.
> I hope you will share with me what is on your mind. I'm ready to listen.

This step may be one of the most difficult steps for most couples. Why? Quite often, the spouse who is complaining exaggerates some of what they are saying because they are emotional. It is also likely that their complaint is sprinkled with other frustrations or stressors. As a result, it is very difficult to listen without interrupting to tell your spouse that they are wrong about how they are describing the situation.

For example, think of customer Bob who is upset not only about his broken appliance, he also had a bad day at work, has a headache from seasonal allergies, and don't forget the baby crying in the background. So, while he is complaining he wrongly states that XYZ Appliances was a month late delivering the dishwasher (even though it was actually two weeks late). Maria overlooks the exaggeration and focuses on the overall message that Bob is irritated about slow service in the first place and the current situation, a broken dishwasher. She is looking at Bob's account and she can see that the dishwasher was actually two weeks late instead of a month, but she does not interrupt to correct him. Instead, she listens to the overall message that Bob feels that he received slow service as a first inconvenience, and that now he has a broken appliance as a second inconvenience.

It is very difficult and certainly an act of "service and honor" to your relationship, if you are able to overlook some of the exaggerations and frustrations expressed by your mate. Listen for the overall message of what your husband or wife is telling you. During this step, I highly recommend that you do not interrupt or correct the accuracy of your mate's statements - even if he or she is exaggerating or does not have all of the facts straight. Instead, focus on hearing what the overall complaint is. Filter out and put aside any irritants or exaggerations that your spouse says. Stripping the emotions from the complaint will often assist you in moving towards stabilizing the conversation.

Do not misinterpret this step. While your mate is talking, I am not advising you to search for a mute button in order to avoid the noise. It is important to listen to everything your spouse says, in order to pass the knowledge check at the end of the conversation. So when she says, "Honey, you weren't listening to a thing I was saying," you can say "Yes, I was listening. And I understand. What I am hearing you say, sugar pudding, is _____."

After your spouse is finished speaking and there has been a pause, move to MarriageBiz Step 3.

MarriageBiz Step 3: Reflective Listening, "What I Am Hearing You Say Is ..."

The excellent customer service representative, after listening to an upset customer (who might even be yelling at them), will calmly say "What I'm hearing you say is _____." For example, Maria might say to customer Bob "OK, what I am hearing is that you are really unhappy that this dishwasher broke and you are now being inconvenienced, especially after you were inconvenienced waiting for the dishwasher to deliver. Is this right?" Bob then says "Yes." He feels Maria understands him. He also feels relieved because he was able to complain and get everything off his chest. His anger and emotions are now down to a 2. Because Maria has diffused the emotions, Bob is now able to focus on negotiating a resolution with XYZ Appliances.

In a marriage relationship, the temptation after your spouse has been complaining is to either correct them on one of their exaggerations or tell them the solution to their problem. However, it is likely that your spouse is still somewhat emotional or even angry, so if you want to negotiate a resolution, it is important that you first complete MarriageBiz Step 3. Using reflective listening will continue to diffuse negative emotions, and it will let your spouse know that you acknowledge and fully understand their complaint. Reflective listening further sets the stage for proper resolution.

There are different ways to conduct reflective listening. One of the most common methods is to say, "What I am hearing you say is _____. Did I get this right?"

Here are some other possible phrases you can use to engage in reflective listening:

➢ "It seems that what you want me to understand is _____. Is this right?"
➢ "If I understand you correctly, the message you are trying to communicate is _____. Am I correct?"
➢ "So, your concern is _____. Am I getting this right?"

I recommend that you come up with your own phrase that you use for reflective listening. Make your response your mantra. You will look like Johnny On The Spot with your reflective listening response. Practice using it with your coworkers, with your customers, with your friends, and with your kids. Then when your spouse is mad at you (one of the most difficult times to remember to do reflective listening), it will be habitual for you to say, "Oh, what I'm hearing you say is _____. Did I get this right?"

If you get it right, you will see your mate's body language start to change. Their frustration is being soothed as they hear you repeat back to them the message they want you to understand.

If you did not get it right, your spouse will feel better that you are trying to understand. In this case, the best thing is to ask your mate to tell you what you did not get right.

Sometimes you may have to try two, three, or four times before you fully understand your spouse's complaint. Keep trying to say, "So, your concern is _____. Am I getting this right?" until your mate says, "YES." Until you hear "YES," you have not finished this step. When you do, then you can move to MarriageBiz Step 4.

MarriageBiz Step 4: Ask what will resolve your spouse's concern.

Imagine Bob complaining to Maria at XYZ Appliances, and she says, "Bob, I tell you what I am going to do. I am going to send you another copy of the instruction manual so you can figure out how to repair your machine. We are too busy selling appliances over here at XYZ." WHAT? Bob is thinking, "You didn't even ask me or take into consideration what I wanted to resolve the problem!" The response that might come out of Bob's mouth next could make some people's ears bleed. A new copy of the instructional manual was NOT what Bob had in mind to resolve his problem.

Fortunately, most business service representatives like Maria are trained to say, "Bob, what can I do to resolve your concern?"

You'd be surprised how rare it is for couples to ask this question of each other. My observation is that husbands often jump to fixing the problem by saying, "I know. I'll do this." The wife, on the other hand, becomes furious because her husband's offer to fix the problem equates to XYZ appliances saying they will send out a new instruction manual which is not the resolution that Bob was looking for!

Again, there is some good intent to fix a problem, but the rush to resolution is damaging. Look, if you tell your spouse how you are going to fix the problem, your heart is headed in the right direction. You are earnestly attempting to make your wife or husband happy. But you are not doing it in the best way! If you want to please your husband or wife, ask your mate "What will resolve this for you?"

This can be asked in a variety of ways, such as:

- Baby, what can I say or do to resolve this concern for you?
- What can I say or do to make you feel better?
- Honey, is there something I can say or do to comfort you, besides listening?
- Do you have any ideas about what I can say or do that would fix this for you?
- Are you able to tell me what you think would resolve this for you?
- Well, I really made a mistake, what can I do to make it up to you?

Asking "What will resolve this for you?" is an extremely powerful question, [16] but it can only be asked after you've done the previous steps, which all take care of the other person's emotions – and set the stage for negotiating a resolution.

There is a good chance your spouse may not have taken the time to identify what resolution they are ideally looking for. Asking this question helps them to start thinking in the direction of resolution. Or, if your spouse has unfairly assumed that you don't care about resolving the matter, then asking "What will resolve this for you?" will hopefully change their mind.

This step starts to shift the conversation towards a resolution. If your spouse does not have any answers for the above, you can give them some time to think about it. Or if you have a suggestion about how to resolve the issue, you can say, "I have a suggestion. Can I tell you what it is?"

Some possible resolutions that are the most common in romantic relationships are:

> An apology.

---

[16] This process is part of "conversation repair" which is an attempt to de-escalate the negativity of the complaint via an apology, a simple smile, or humor.

> A new agreement that prevents the same problem from happening in the future.[17]
> Words of reassurance about anything that might make your partner feel better.
> Some action that makes your partner feel important in order to "make up for" or overcome a previous mistake that you made in the relationship. [18] (Think of a restaurant manager giving you free appetizers and drinks because they messed up your dinner order).
> An agreement to receive help from a professional or an outside source regarding a problem that you are having. For example, if there is a

---

[17] Inghilleri and Solomon (2010) point out that "for some customers, the most valuable compensation isn't material. Some customers respond more positively to a chance to help improve your company. These customers want most of all to help make your service better, protect future customers from similar wrongs, or feel assured that their advice is important to you."

[18] Inghillleri and Solomon (2010) encourage five-star businesses to provide something *extra* during recovery from a problem. This is a key principle in fixing a problem, and it helps to resolve the customer's sense of injustice of having been wronged or let down. There is a list on page 34 and 35 of Exceptional Service Exceptional Profit called "How Should You Compensate a Customer for a Service or Product Failure?" Some of the MarriageBiz principles for romantic relationships echo this list.

financial problem, you might agree to see a financial consultant.

You have now essentially entered the negotiations for a resolution. Sometimes resolution comes very quickly. Your spouse suggests a resolution that you think is reasonable. You quickly agree and the problem is solved.[19] Other times, the negotiation process can take some time and energy. If you start to get impatient while you are going through negotiations, I recommend that you think about how much time and energy it consumes to quarrel without reaching resolution.

MarriageBiz Step 5: Negotiate a resolution with your spouse.

Try to imagine Bob asking Maria for a fully paid vacation because his dishwasher is broken. Hmmmm....Maria is undoubtedly not authorized to give out vacation packages in exchange for broken dishwashers. If the customer is asking for an unreasonable resolution, then the business service

---

[19] Being open to compromise and "accepting your partner's influence" can drastically change the way you and your partner handle conflict (Gottman, Gottman, & DeClaire, 2006).

representative will usually suggest some alternative resolutions. For example, Maria might offer Bob a repair person to fix the dishwasher within 24 hours at no cost to him. Or she might offer to give him a new dishwasher within a week with installation at no cost. Because of the inconvenience, she might also offer to give him a free gift card or a $100 refund on his original purchase to make up for the mistake and the inconvenience.

Likewise, it is possible that your spouse might ask for a resolution that you think is completely unreasonable. What do you do if your spouse wants the sun, and the moon, and the stars? If this happens, start with the positive and again remind them that you want to resolve their concern, but you are unable to complete the resolution they are requesting. At this point, it is a good idea to think of one or more reasonable resolutions to offer them. Hopefully, your spouse will accept your offer and you will agree on a resolution even though it may take more than one offer to resolve the matter. If you follow all of the above steps and you think that your spouse is repeatedly and regularly unreasonable (problems do not get resolved as a result) then you may start to wonder if you are the unreasonable partner in the relationship. In this case, you can seek out professional advice from a marriage or family expert on whether you are being reasonable or not. Or, you might ask a couple of trusted friends their opinion.

We offer a service at www.marriagebizonline.com where we conduct relationship coaching via e-mail. For a fee, you can visit my website and can submit a question by emailing marriagebizonline@gmail.com. Either myself or a trained MarriageBiz coach will give you an expert opinion on the matter! We will make every effort to reply back to your question within 24 hours.

What do you do if you keep offering various suggestions for resolution, and your mate does not like any of them? Additionally, your mate has not offered any resolution. Just let them know that you want to resolve the matter, and once they've come up with some suggestions for resolution, to revisit your relationship service counter!

If the problem still does not get resolved, I would suggest that you take it seriously. You may want to consider MarriageBiz coaching or a session of marriage therapy in order to resolve the problem. Not resolving a problem leads to an insecure relationship that is headed down a collision course!

MarriageBiz Step 6: Ask your mate if you have fully resolved their concern.

After customer Bob and business representative Maria have agreed upon a resolution, she asks Bob, "Bob, have I completely resolved this concern?" "Have I resolved all your concerns? Is there anything else I can do for you today?" Trained service representatives are taught to ask the customer this at the very end of the conversation. They are taught to not assume that the customer's complaint has been fully resolved until they have asked the questions and heard the customer say that the complaint has been resolved.

When the business representative takes a moment to make sure that the complaint is fully resolved, the customer again feels valued and satisfied with their transaction. Typically, the customer will continue conducting business with this company. That is, even though the business made a mistake or there was a problem in the business relationship, trust has been restored and the business relationship continues.

All businesses make mistakes. It is how businesses rectify the situation that truly differentiates one business from another.

Likewise, in a marriage relationship, I highly recommend that you ask your husband or wife, "Do you feel better? Have I resolved your concern? Is it okay if we start dinner now?"[20] Asking your spouse if the complaint has been resolved seals the deal. It makes your spouse feel special, secure, and satisfied. Although you made a mistake or there was a problem, trust and security have been restored and the romantic relationship can resume.[21]

In a business setting, it is always a good idea to proactively follow-up a few days or weeks later.

---

[20] Some of the complaints that you receive in the relationship service department will likely be the result of "perpetual issues," those that continue to arise because of differences in personality or perspective. Creating a healthy dialogue will allow you both to make peace with these issues so that they can be addressed in future conflict discussions, even if the resolution is simply "I respect and understand that you have a different point of view."

[21] 69% of marital problems can be classified as "never ending" better known as "perpetual issues" (issues due to differences in personality or perspective). Finding some sort of resolution, even temporarily, can help two people with personality differences still have a satisfying relationship based on trust and security. Coming to a resolution sends the message that you value and respect your spouse, which makes it easier to then accept each other's differences.

Successful business representatives will often follow-up with their customers. They check-in to make sure the customer is satisfied with the follow-through on the resolution. They ask the customer: Do you think that we are doing what we said we were going to do to resolve your concern? [22]

In marriage, you can do the same thing. A few days or a couple weeks after you have resolved your spouse's concerns, ask your spouse: "From your perspective, do you think I have followed-through on our new agreement?"

---

[22] Inghilleri and Solomon (2010) document the importance of business follow-up after there has been a customer service problem and a repair. The purpose of the follow-up is to ensure customer satisfaction with the customer service repair.

Chapter 5

Refrain From Jumping Over the Relationship Service Desk

Imagine the following scenario: Jim walks up to the customer service desk at his local cable company. He states his complaint is that his cable box has not been working properly and that it needs to be replaced. He also complains that he missed part of the football game as a result of the cable not working. Jane, the cable customer service representative pulls up Jim's account. Then Jane jumps over the customer service desk and says, "Yeah, well you were late on a payment two months ago." Jane is now making her own complaint and both Jane and Jim are on the same side of the customer service counter. No one is servicing anyone else's complaint. The customer service counter has basically lost its identity and has completely shut down. The result is that no one's complaints will be heard and no resolutions will be made.

Not very effective. Now Jim is furious because he knows for a fact that Jane could care less that he missed watching the football game on his only day off.

He makes a sarcastic comment to Jane and pretty soon they are both bickering.

Believe it or not, this scenario is one of the most common pitfalls I see with troubled couples who are having conflict on a regular basis. In essence, both husband and wife are hanging out in front of the service counter bickering. No one is staying behind the relationship service counter long enough to resolve any complaints.

If you want a happy marriage, when your spouse complains, I am recommending the following:

In all circumstances, NO MATTER WHAT, please refrain from jumping over the relationship service counter! Stay behind the service counter and service your partner's complaint.

This means that when your spouse makes a complaint, you will have to stop yourself from thinking about your own complaints in the relationship.

Take a minute and think about how you normally react when your partner makes complaints. These are some common examples of *unhelpful* thoughts that people sometimes have when their spouse makes a complaint:

> "I can't believe she is complaining. I am a much more helpful husband than Mary's husband."
> "Do I have to get everything right? I do this right. I do that right. Now I make a mistake, and I have to hear about it."
> "What the heck? I was mad at her on Tuesday. I just didn't say anything about it because I was trying to be the bigger person. Now, I'm really going to let her have it."
> "If she wants to pick a fight, I can fight. Bring it on."

These thoughts are not conducive to the MarriageBiz Service Attitudes in Chapter 2, and these kind of negative thoughts tend to lead to the following defensive reactions:

> Comparing yourself to someone who is behaving worse. This is deflecting the attention off of you and onto someone else. In this case, you are complaining that your spouse is not being appreciative.
> Complaining that your spouse is being too critical because you do so many things right.

➢ Complaining about a behavior that you do not like about your spouse.

➢ Taking a defensive approach by thinking of ways to combat her complaints.

In all of these cases, I urge you to consider if you would have these reactions in a business or work context...most likely not.

In all honesty, I think jumping over the relationship service desk to switch roles is human nature. When your spouse starts to complain about you and something you did wrong, it is naturally going to trigger thoughts about your own marital concerns that are unresolved.[23] A scenario that often occurs in busy families is the following: you have an occurrence where you and your spouse do not see eye to eye on something, but the timing is not right for you to complain. Maybe you are in public. Or perhaps you are eating dinner with your in-laws. Or maybe you are both right in the middle of getting your preschooler and toddler to bed. So, you don't ring the relationship

---

[23] Responding to your spouse's complaint with your own complaint or by defending yourself is called Defensiveness. The Gottmans have identified Defensiveness as one of the "Four Horsemen of the Apocolypse" because it has the potential to escalate in ways that is a predictor for divorce (Gottman, Gottman, & DeClaire, 2006).

service bell. By the time you get home or get the kids in bed, you have focused your attention on something else (hopefully something more pleasurable) and you still have not communicated your complaint. Eventually, something will happen that will trigger your spouse to have a complaint, and they will bring their complaint to the relationship service counter. Suddenly, any and possibly all complaints that you had in the back of your mind are now on the tip of your tongue. If she is going to complain, so are you!

But the fact of the matter is, if you want a secure and trusting relationship – then there can only be one person on the side of the counter that is making the complaint and the other person has to stay on the side of the counter that is servicing the complaint. For example, when your husband starts to complain that he thinks you spent too much money on back to school shopping for the kids and you find yourself thinking about how he spent too much money on his golf game over the summer, you must put that thought aside and revisit it later. He made the complaint about the school supplies budget, so it is important to respectfully find a resolution for that concern. Then, if the entertainment budget and the cost of golf is a concern that you have, by all means you can now bring your complaint to the relationship service desk.

In all fairness, I recommend that if your spouse brings up a relationship complaint, please service their complaint first - all the way from MarriageBiz Step 1 through MarriageBiz Step 6. Then, after you have completed the MarriageBiz steps, you can then ask your spouse to reverse roles by telling them that you also have a complaint.

Actually, sometimes you may attempt to go to the relationship service desk when your spouse is at work, in public, or in front of the kids. But you tend to not get a good response because in reality your spouse cannot effectively handle your complaint while they are at work, making decisions on what kind of produce to get at the market, or juggling your children's needs. So, I recommend that you wait until it is a good time and your spouse can readily sit behind the relationship service desk and properly handle your complaint.

Another reason that people sometimes jump over the relationship service desk is because they are less in tune with relationship problems than their spouse. In other words, some spouses are not really thinking about relationship problems until their partner starts to complain about a relationship problem. For example, research shows that most women are socialized to spend more time thinking about family and personal relationships whereas most men are socialized to think more about competition and being a good provider at work. So, it makes sense that women bring up more complaints about romantic and family relationships than men. However, when wives complain, then husbands will often change the channel in their head and tune into the relationship problems. The husband then jumps over the customer service counter and makes his complaints known as well.

I am asking spouses to refrain from jumping over the relationship service desk. If you were too busy to previously register a complaint, or if you were distracted and not tuned into the relationship problems channel, it is still important for you to stay on the right side of the relationship service counter when your wife registers her complaint. Then, when you have finished servicing her complaint, you can then focus on what your complaints are and ask your spouse to service them.

Husbands - here is some news that may help you! If your wife brings up more complaints than you do, you do not need to compete with her! It is not a competition to see who can come up with more complaints.[24] The "bring it on" attitude resolves nothing. If she complains about you more than you complain about her, it does not mean that you are a less worthy partner, less wonderful, or less special. It simply means that she probably naturally shifts to thinking about the marriage relationship more often than you do, and therefore she is going to have more complaints. Women are also more likely to spend time studying "how to" self-help books (like this one), magazine articles, and blogs to inform themselves on how to have a successful family life.

For this reason, I am seriously trying to keep this book short and to the point for you men who typically do not read self-help books. MarriageBiz is also a good resource for those men who might feel that they do not need help. MarriageBiz might change their mind.

Men, if you service her complaints, she will feel satisfied and secure. If you have complaints that you forgot about because you are more inclined to focus your attention on the NFL or the stock market, then by

---

[24] Such an environment will create more defensiveness. Counterattacking or attempting to defend yourself by jumping at the chance to criticize the person with the complaint will not help if you are both still in the business of maintaining and strengthening your relationship.

all means bring up your complaints after you have finished resolving hers. But, if you don't have any complaints about her, don't try to create one just to show her that you are equally as good as her. Most women do not bring up complaints to be better than their husbands. They bring up complaints because they have a concern they feel is legitimate and they want it resolved. For many women, just like at the customer service counter, they want to feel valued at the relationship service counter so they can proceed with their shopping!

Chapter 6
MarriageBiz Strategies

MarriageBiz Strategy 1: Tell Your Spouse Often That You Want to Make Them Happy, and Remind Them To Bring Their Complaints To You.

Have you ever noticed that many stores' customer service signs used to be small and the counters were tucked away in the back corner of the store? Nowadays, when you walk into a business, you will often see the Customer Service sign right in the front. Many stores have changed the accessibility of the customer service counter for more reasons than one. One reason is that having a customer service department in the front of the store is basically inviting customers to bring complaints when they have them.

A second reason is because businesses want to make it more convenient for customers to get complaints serviced. The business realizes that if a customer is coming to the customer service counter, that they may already be inconvenienced. The business does not want the customer to search for the Customer Service counter at the back of the store, because this will likely add to the customer's frustration and escalate the problem.

Likewise, I encourage you to make relationship service easy for your mate. Remind them often that your relationship service counter is available to take complaints. In other words, flash the RELATIONSHIP SERVICE sign often during the start of spending time together. In addition, some of the following strategies below can help to make the servicing of complaints more convenient for your mate.

MarriageBiz Strategy 2: Plan the Hours When Your Relationship Service Counter Will Be Open

People sometimes complain that their spouse brings up complaints at very poor times - such as at night when they are trying to go to sleep. You know what I am talking about, the kind of conversations that can seriously lead to sleep deprivation. Another scenario I can think of is when I had at least three husbands with busy careers who complained during marriage therapy that their wife would call them with relationship service complaints while they were at work! When counseling with these couples, I quickly identified that the wife did not know when her husband's service department was and was not open. So her frustration grew and she just kept trying to ring the relationship service bell, even while her husband was at work. I also want to point out that these types of situations can also occur when both spouses work, or even when the woman is the primary breadwinner in the marriage.

While conducting marriage counseling, I have noticed that some couples are not only fighting about parenting, money, or sex – they are now fighting about *when* to fight! Of course, one of the best ways to *not* fight is to have your spouse trust that you have a regularly open and skilled relationship service department. Try this: when your husband or wife comes to you in order to have a complaint serviced, even if it is an inconvenient time, stop and resolve the complaint via MarriageBiz Steps from Chapter 4. Ask what will resolve your spouse's concern. After you have successfully resolved their complaint, you have now developed greater trust in the relationship! Your spouse trusts you to service his or her complaints, so now he or she is more likely to wait for your service department to be open in the future.

Tell your spouse when your relationship service counter is open to receive complaints.

Most disgruntled people, whether spouses or consumers, can wait for the service counter to open, if only they know when the counter will be open. Businesses are accustomed to conveying to consumers when their customer service department or counter is open. Businesses recognize that this is an important part of a trusting relationship. Likewise, your marriage will benefit if, for example, you tell your spouse that you can best service complaints between 8-10 p.m. (after the kids are in bed but before you are too tired to discuss the matter).

I recommend that you primarily take complaints when you are in a good position to do so. In business, sometimes a sales person will knowingly take an adversarial call from a disgruntled client when the sales person is really not in a position to be able to address the customer's concern. At that moment, it is important for the business person to make a decision on whether the timing is right to take a call. I am not saying to blow off the customer! What I am saying is that sometimes it may be better for a business person to wait just a little while until they are positioned properly with additional facts to address the situation. Furthermore, with businesses requiring their employees to multi-task, it is a smart move for the sales person to make sure he can give a disgruntled customer his undivided attention. If a disgruntled customer leaves a message asking the sales person to return the call, sometimes it is better to wait. Preparing mentally and practically is a smart move.

In marriage, couples also find themselves multi-tasking. However, I recommend that you choose times to open your relationship service counter when you are not stressed or multi-tasking. For example, it is good to choose a time of day when you are not too tired, hungry, or distracted. There is an acronym known as HALT that mental health professionals frequently use in addictions counseling. HALT reminds addicts who are in recovery to stop and take a break when they are Hungry, Angry, Lonely, or Tired. I think HALT also applies to servicing and making marriage complaints. If you or your spouse are Hungry, Angry, Lonely, or Tired; it is not a good time for a marriage meeting to bring up and service complaints.

You and your spouse will benefit from knowing when your relationship service counter is open.

However, if your spouse knocks at your relationship service door outside of the regular relationship service hours you've identified, then I would suggest still servicing their complaint if at all possible. For example, when a crisis or other unplanned event happens, I recommend that you try to respond quickly. The more prompt you are at taking care of problems, the sooner you regain a trusting and secure relationship that is more pleasurable, happy, and fulfilling.

In some cases, your spouse may have a complaint regarding when your relationship service counter is open or closed. If this happens, then you may consider resolving that complaint by adjusting your relationship service hours. Keep in mind that it is important for you to identify a time that is good for both you and your spouse. Otherwise, when your spouse complains it might remind you of fingernails on a chalk board. Imagine a business that you need customer service attention from telling you that the customer service department is only open between 3 and 5 a.m.! Or, that the only time they are open is between 3 and 5 p.m. when you have to pick up the kids from school, drive them to activities, and then cook dinner. Quite simply, it would be extremely inconvenient, if not impossible, for you to go to that business's customer service counter. You just might start conducting your business elsewhere.

Similarly, it is important for your marriage relationship to negotiate times that are good for both of you as to when the relationship service counter will be open. Servicing complaints is work – it is not the fun, pleasurable part of your relationship – and it takes time, so try to pick a time when it is convenient and comfortable for both of you.

Businesses, by in large, have really improved by giving the customer some kind of an idea of when they will be servicing a complaint. For example, now when you call customer service, you are often told how long you will have to wait or how many people are ahead of you in line. Businesses have become smarter in this way. In the corporate world, customers who have registered a complaint via e-mail will often get a reply telling them what the timeline is for getting a response. Generally, people like to know a business has received their complaint and that the business has a time scheduled to address it. Ultimately, this instills a sense of security in customers.

Communicating with your spouse regarding when your service counter will be open or what timeline works for addressing his or her complaint is a good idea. When you give your husband or wife a timeline, you are essentially giving them a carrot, something to hold on to. Then, as long as you follow-through with actually servicing the complaint within this timeline, you can optimize using your service skills. Being able to focus solely on your partner's complaints, leads to better outcomes and resolution.

MarriageBiz Strategy 3: Put Out the "Relationship Service" Bell.

Sometimes a customer is sending signals to a sales person that they are not happy. The sales person, however, is not picking up the vibe. Instead, they are too focused on closing the next deal. Successful businesses make a point of having a customer service bell at their counter - in addition to having a specific phone number and procedures for customers to make complaints.

When I observe couples, I notice that sometimes one person is expressing a message to their spouse that they are annoyed. But somehow their spouse is not registering it in their mind as "This is a complaint that I need to service." Therefore, they fail to take the proper steps and pretty soon a small problem has developed into a catastrophe!

I recommend that it is important to put out a relationship service bell at your counter! To do this, speak with your wife or husband and help choose a method for alerting you that they are seeking for you to service a complaint! I have asked many couples to do this in counseling and each couple has come up with their own strategy. For example, one couple I was working with would say, "Not to start a fight, but....." Using these words was their way of letting the other person know they were ringing the bell and they were now standing in front of the relationship service counter. Another couple I saw in counseling liked the customer service metaphor so much that they started saying, "Is the customer service counter open right now? I have a complaint."

I can honestly say that sometimes I am guilty of not noticing when my husband is registering his complaint at the service counter. Sometimes Brendan will be expressing his thoughts about something but it does not register in my mind that he is looking to have a complaint serviced. Obviously, I am pretty alert to servicing relationship complaints since I am writing a book about it. I say this to make the point that I do this for a living, and sometimes I still do not recognize that my spouse is trying to register a complaint.

This is why it helps to have a relationship service bell! Your "bell" can be a word, a phrase, or a signal. But, I do recommend that you pay attention and provide good service when you hear the service bell ring because this is essential to having a successful marriage.

MarriageBiz Strategy 4: Complete Regular Research About Your Mate

Besides providing good customer service, you will notice that a good business invests in research and development regarding the products and services that appeal to their customers. And they don't stop conducting research after they attract a customer. The consumer research is ongoing as the needs and wishes of their customers change with time.

Likewise, let me suggest that it is important to regularly engage in research to figure out what your wife or husband likes. Pay attention to the following: What do they wish for? What do they say that they hope for? When they are angry, what do they complain about and how can you fix it? Are there needs that your partner has that you are not meeting? Ask your mate what services you engage in during the relationship that he or she likes and continue those services. Ask your spouse what services he or she wishes you provided that you either forget to do or need to learn. Develop yourself in such a way that you are pleasing to your mate.

I cannot stress this enough. Often, one part of a relationship can be great enough to attract a mate. However, if a person's overall needs and wishes are not researched, developed, and provided, the relationship is still at greater risk of falling apart.

After completing research, praise your partner for the things that are most important to them *and to you.* If a supervisor tells an employee that they like what they are doing, it often motivates that employee to do things more routinely and possibly even improve their procedures. The same is true in marriage. Notice, appreciate, and praise what you like about your partner. Complimenting your significant other will likely motivate them to make the behaviors you like more routine and habitual.

MarriageBiz Strategy 5: Scratch Each Other's Backs

That's right. You've most likely participated in the business philosophy of "you scratch my back, and I'll scratch yours" or you've possibly seen it in the movies. Either way, the idea is a good one in business relationships. It refers to a mutual contract of both people obtaining what they want from the other person. Given the divorce rate, it seems like maybe we need to do a little more mutual spousal back scratching. Give it a try! When your partner makes a complaint, this is actually the perfect opportunity for you to figure out where and how they want their back scratched. Once you figure it out, by all means do the scratching. It might be a small itch, in an area of their back they can't reach without your help, one that needs to be scratched quickly – just like small complaints.

Unfortunately, some people have had poor role modeling when it comes to back scratching. For example, in our grandparents generation, if a husband did not scratch his wife's back there was not a whole lot she could do about it. Because of this, men today are sometimes behaving the way their fathers or grandfathers did, except they are not recognizing that the consequence of not back scratching could lead divorce nowadays. The majority of today's couples are looking for a mutual contract and a mutual partnership. So, if she went with you to the football game, which is not really her favorite thing to do, then she thinks she is scratching your back.

Next month, she asks you to go to the ballet, and she is likely to get angry if you say "no way!" Your reaction to her request might be one in which she were trying to force you to wear a tutu. No worries, most women don't want to see their man dressed in a tutu, although it could be humorous. At this point, I recommend that it is only fair for you to scratch her back, which means going to the ballet, because she scratched yours.

In business, this concept of mutual back-scratching is also sometimes referred to as a win-win. In win-win relationships, both sides put on the table their priority needs. Ideally, they negotiate an agreement and a relationship that benefits the priority needs of both parties. Our definition of a win-win does not necessarily mean that either party in the business relationship obtains everything they want. To the contrary, win-win is a result that occurs when both parties are effectively able to negotiate an agreement which they feel will mutually benefit their organizations.

Let's revert back to the football/ballet example. In some relationships, I have observed that when a spouse requests to go on a date to the ballet or to watch a football game, their mate says "No." Perhaps because I am so intent on the business concept of back-scratching, I am usually shocked to observe one spouse outright denying the other person's request.

In this example, imagine that a husband says, "But honey, you *know* I don't like going to the ballet." His wife then starts complaining about how she doesn't really like football; however she goes with him to the local pub to watch football with his friends and their wives. I have observed in some cases, for example, the husband again saying, "But honey, you know I don't like going to the ballet." The problem here is that this husband is missing the point – he is not recognizing the importance of back scratching!

I vividly remember a couple in marriage therapy where the husband complained that his wife would not watch the Steelers football games with him. This really angered him because he loved football. He commented that his friends' wives put on their jerseys and put out popcorn and nachos and watched the game with their husband. He had decided this was important to him in his marriage. He was a very hard worker and took his wife to church on Sundays and helped her with household chores. Churchgoing was more her deal than his, but he attended almost every weekend with her. Furthermore, he helped her with household chores every weekend to free up time to watch the game. He felt very strongly that he was scratching her back, and he was indignant that she would not scratch his. She would exclaim "But, baby, you know I hate football."

It is at these moments when a business lesson is a very good idea. In the above example, I encouraged the wife to negotiate times to watch football games with her husband each season. In business contracts and relationships, the fact is that there is always a mutually beneficial contract that includes back scratching.[25]

---

[25] Women are more likely to compromise or be influenced by what their husbands want. Men can sometimes feel threatened by compromise because it feels like they will be relinquishing some of their power in the relationship. To the contrary, the ability to come to a compromise can raise the amount of power, respect, and appreciation the husband has in his marriage relationship (Gottman, Gottman, & DeClaire, 2006). According to MarriageBiz, business relationships use compromise as a way to earn greater respect, power, and appreciation in the business world. Likewise, the same is true in the world of marriage.

Anyone who tells themselves that a romantic relationship does not include a mutually beneficial contract is taking a huge risk of potential failure. It's possible that your partner might continue to stay and scratch your back even if you don't scratch theirs. However, if you love your partner and want to keep the relationship, this is a gamble you might not want to take!

Sadly, I have witnessed some wives or husbands who unknowingly gambled away their marriage. Basically, they did not service their partner's complaints, did not complete relationship research, and did not scratch their partner's back. They came in for counseling *after* their husband or wife had already moved out and moved on. They want to know what to do different in their next relationship so that they have success as opposed to divorce.

There are no guarantees, but if you notice during courtship that your partner takes care of your complaints and if you notice that you can generally service your partner's complaints and resolve them; then you have the beginning of a trusting, secure relationship that can work through problems and conflict. If you haven't been together long enough to figure that out, then I would suggest not going into a partnership with that person until you do. I assume you wouldn't commit to doing business at the same location for the next fifty years without knowing if that business has a good customer service department complete with excellent back-scratching. Likewise, it is never a good idea to commit to a romantic relationship for the next fifty years until you have great trust in your partner's relationship service and back-scratching.

Once you have committed to a certain contract of mutual back-scratching in your romantic relationship, it is important not to manipulate or change the contract. When you make your agreement, discuss it long enough so that it is clear and concise. Then, it is important that you follow-through on your end of the agreement. The breech of contractual obligations can lead to significant complications in your current and future agreements.

MarriageBiz Strategy 6: Plan times for regular meetings.

Businesses have regular budget meetings, planning meetings, review meetings, and retreats for team-building. At these meetings, there is a purpose or an agenda stated at the beginning. The meeting stays focused on the purpose and the agenda. If you want a successful marriage, the same should be true of your marriage conversations. If you want to have a conversation with your husband, try telling him what the purpose is at the beginning. If the purpose is to have fun and connect after a long day, explain that your agenda is to connect and enjoy each other's company. Does he agree with the agenda? Since women often initiate conversations and meetings, I urge you to get your husband's agreement on the agenda ahead of time. You are far more likely to have a successful discussion or transaction with your mate when you do this.

I recommend that you plan times for regular meetings in your marriage as well.[26] Try scheduling a monthly budget meeting. Brendan is the leader on this in our marriage relationship. We sit down and review our expenses from the previous month and our projected expenses for the next couple of months.

I also encourage you to have weekly or monthly planning meetings. Discuss what is on the calendar, as

---

[26] Dr. Curtis of The Business of Love also recommends budget meetings, review meetings, and planning meetings and retreats for your couple's relationship (Curtis, 2006).

to who is responsible for which tasks, and how you will accomplish your goals. During planning meetings, you can also check-up on any emotional concerns your partner may be having.

Frequent meetings are opportunities to give feedback to your partner about previous agreements you have made regarding responsibilities, budget, and other issues. During these meetings, start with the positive and show appreciation. Then discuss any concerns you may have. This is similar to a business setting where an employee at the bottom of the corporate ladder might not receive appreciation until their supervisor conducts an annual review. However, this employee needs to feel appreciated between reviews and be given room for growth. Otherwise, they will not perform to expectations or are more likely to leave and work somewhere else where they are appreciated.

Chapter 7

Breaking Cycles of Helplessness

If you have failed in your relationships in the past or have concern that your current relationship is failing, I would urge you to think about whether you are creating a situation where your partner feels helpless. On the other hand, perhaps you service your partner's complaints, but you feel helpless in getting your concerns serviced by your spouse.

There are many ways to hold power over someone else and to make them feel helpless or small. One way is to beat someone up physically. Another way is to deny someone things they need to survive, such as money for basic necessities or to keep them from friends, creating isolation. Finally, another way is to dismiss and ignore someone's concerns.

I realize that if you have not been servicing your spouse's complaints properly, there is a good chance that your intention was not to cause feelings of helplessness. I have noticed that many people do not think of it in this way, but *if you are not regularly servicing many of your spouse's complaints, then you likely are causing them to feel helpless and mentally harming them.* In many cases, you are the only person to whom your spouse can turn to have certain needs met. If you choose not to service many of your spouse's complaints and give them the desires of their heart, you are holding power over them. You are making your partner feel small, helpless, and unimportant which may have the same kind of long-term effects as physical battering.

The long term effects of not resolving many of your spouse's complaints are feelings of insecurity, fear, anxiety, confusion, and helplessness. Having helpless feelings on a regular basis within a marriage relationship can contribute to your partner having depression, panic disorder, tearfulness, irritability and anger, substance use and abuse or other addictions, distrust of you and others, infidelities, and divorce. [27]

If you don't believe me, then just think about trying to do business where you can't get a complaint serviced.

---

[27] Increasing relationship service will decrease feelings of helplessness in families. This is important because helplessness in family relationships creates risks for mental health disorders, teenage defiance, substance abuse and addictions, and criminal behavior. Our society will benefit from good examples of relationship service in marriage.

How do you feel when the business refuses to service your complaint even after several attempts?

> Do you feel valuable or do you feel unimportant? Likely you feel unimportant. The more times you have tried to get your complaint serviced, the more devalued you believe you are to the business.

> Do you feel frustrated and angry? Most likely, the longer you wait for your complaint to be serviced, the more angry and frustrated you become.

> Do you trust the business will honor you or do you start wondering if they are cheating you in some other kind of way? (I believe it is normal to question a business's overall agenda when you are not serviced correctly or in a timely fashion).

> Do you want to continue this business relationship or do you think about conducting business somewhere else?

When you promised to love and honor your mate, you were also promising to serve them. You were promising to take care of them – that means that you are responsible for making sure that you do not make them feel helpless on a regular basis. This means you will honor and service most of their reasonable complaints.

If you are unsure whether your spouse is being unreasonable about one of their complaints and suggestions for resolution, then you can certainly contact a MarriageBiz coach to get an opinion via www.marriagebizonline.com. For a fee, you can visit my website and submit an e-mail advice question to marriagebizonline@gmail.com. We will make every attempt to get back to you within 24 hours.

I believe it is impossible for a person to acknowledge and service all complaints. No business can immediately service all complaints nor can any human being. However, it is reasonable to expect our partner to value us enough to service our complaints the majority of the time when their relationship service department is open.

Here is what amazes me. There are a whole lot of well-meaning, spiritual, good people who have amazing intentions for their marriage, but they are unintentionally psychologically harming their spouse because they do not have a functioning, skilled relationship service department.

The scenarios and steps in Chapters 2 – 6 may not seem that challenging at first glance. But putting them into practice IS very difficult. We sometimes find it hard to have humility, to listen patiently, to behave kindly, and to serve others.

When you use MarriageBiz to effectively service your partners' complaints, not only are you refraining from mentally battering them and creating helplessness, you are doing the exact opposite. You create a respectful, caring relationship - a bond that is very close. Your partner feels that you value them. They trust you are in this together and willing to fix problems. They can see that you are humble and unselfish.

We need a new way to go about marriage. Although the expectation to stay married still exists, the norm has changed drastically in the past fifty years. I think that many Americans have an attitude of service and humility. We are just failing to apply this attitude to marriage. We need some additional skill sets and behaviors for today's marriage. Today's couples are regularly going to the service counter complaining for mutually contractual partnerships. So, we need the business skill sets to take care of those complaints.

Ironically, the skill sets that are required in marriage really are spiritual (mutual service and humility); they are also the kind of skills that good businesses engage in with their customers. Let's take these skill sets behind closed doors into our homes. When we do, then America really can thrive that much more – we will have a more secure home base!

Also, by modeling MarriageBiz, we can teach our children an example of relationship service that may help them raise great children who are better able to serve not only our families, but potentially better serve our community, economy, military, and government. Relationship service modeled in the marriage and family relationship will give children and adults the practice they need to be more productive workers and employees. Likewise, better service to our country and our economy can lead to more prosperity for future generations to come.

What to Do If Your Spouse Does Not Have A Relationship Service Counter

If your mate does not have a relationship service counter, you cannot force him or her to have one. This likely makes you feel helpless, frustrated, devalued, and hurt. You can keep making complaints and requests for different service. However, ultimately if your husband or wife refuses to make adjustments, you will have to decide whether you can live under these marital conditions: not being valued and feelings of helplessness are important concerns to get resolved. In these cases, you may have to think about how serious your unresolved marriage concerns are and how important they are to your quality of life.

In some cases, even if your spouse does not effectively resolve your concerns, I would suggest that you try to role model going through the MarriageBiz steps and servicing your spouse's complaints. If you have not been doing a great job resolving your spouse's complaints, then being the first to change this in your marriage will likely breed more security within your relationship. You are basically role modeling the kind of reaction you would like when you make a relationship complaint – then you can ask your mate to repeat the same process when you make a complaint.

Chapter 8

The Joy of Relationship Service Success

I want you to know the joy *and* the profitability of relationship service success! If you have not known what to do when your spouse is complaining about you or upset about a marriage problem, then I believe that following the MarriageBiz steps in this book will inspire you and help you. So many people, men and women, have come to my office with feelings of helplessness. His wife is upset, but he doesn't know what steps to take to fix it. Her husband is angry, but she has no idea where to go next. People want to save their marriage but they keep saying the wrong things and pretty soon their spouse is just *more upset and angry*! Yikes! Usually, I am witnessing the husband or wife saying all kinds of *unhelpful* things. However, I am able to identify that the husband or wife has great intentions of service and love for their family.

I imagine the same for you, and I want you to know the joy of relationship service success! Although it takes humility, work, and skill to service your spouse's complaints, I trust that you know the joy and success that comes from a job well done and the gratification of achievement. I am picturing you, like so many of my clients. You know the joy, profitability, and success of a job well done in another part of your life such as:

- ➢ You are confident at work. You are part of an organization that provides an important service or product to others.
- ➢ You are a wonderful, attentive mother to your children and your home. People tell you that you are a fantastic homemaker.
- ➢ You successfully service and resolve the problems of your customers. Customers write great letters to your boss regarding your service.
- ➢ You proudly and unselfishly serve your country, or your community in the military, law enforcement, or fire and rescue. Saving and protecting lives is gratifying.
- ➢ You heal and teach people via service as a health care provider or you serve as an educator. You love educating our youth.
- ➢ You generously serve your community as a volunteer or minister in your church community. You create a sense of peace in people who are searching for hope and a faith in God.

> You own a business that provides a service to consumers. You watch your business and your profits grow.

In almost all of these roles, you have probably had at least some if not extensive training along with a thorough review of policies and procedures. Or, you have taken the time to read and educate yourself about how to best parent your new baby or how to minister to your church. As a result, you feel competent and confident in yourself. You work hard and when you do a good job, you get compliments from your supervisor and co-workers, along with promotions, higher pay or profits, and respect from colleagues and friends. I certainly hope you realize these joys.

However, even if you have the joys of a job well done in your business, work, civic, or parenting life, you may not have the joy of knowing what kind of profits will ever come from your married life if you do not properly service your partner's complaints.

As I said, servicing the complaints of your spouse requires work, humility, skill, and dedication. However, just like in your business and vocational life, if you apply MarriageBiz principles, you can have numerous profits and successes. I urge you to try the MarriageBiz program for six months to one year. Demonstrate to your partner that you will service his or her complaints and notice how your relationship blossoms, how your partner changes, and how gratifying it can be.

Some likely profits from your hard work at servicing marriage complaints may consist of one or more of the following results:

➢ A happier spouse who feels that you value him or her.

➢ A calmer, more secure spouse.

➢ Less fighting between you and your spouse.

➢ Your spouse having fewer feelings of helplessness, anger, and sadness.

➢ Your spouse learning to better resolve your complaints via your example.

➢ Your spouse bragging to friends and family about how good your marriage is.

➢ Better teamwork in your marriage as you learn to make adjustments that your spouse suggests.

➢ A better sex life with your mate.

➢ Your children witnessing more respect and less fighting.

➢ A more productive spouse at work ($$$) and in the household.

➢ Decreased risk of infidelities and divorce.

➢ Decreased risk for mental health symptoms and substance use problems for yourself, your spouse, and your children.

➢ More personal development and skills (because your spouse will likely complain about your weaknesses and character flaws - and thus lead the way to your self-improvement)!

➢ Breaking the cycle of helplessness in family relationships.

If I have not inspired you during the first seven chapters of MarriageBiz to change your responses to your spouse's complaints, then I hope that this list will motivate you!

People say in marriage that the two shall become one. You are meant to be a team. You agreed to be each other's helpmates and backscratchers. The only way you can truly be a team with your significant other is if you are influenced by them - and make adjustments for and with them. It is especially important to make adjustments when you know your spouse is right.

Sometimes our pride gets in the way. We know our spouse is right, but we are reluctant to say, "Ok, I will work on changing that about myself." Wives and husbands, the only way you can truly be a helpmate is if you make adjustments for your spouse. When your mate has certain reasonable expectations that you know would make your life together better, then you ought to make those adjustments.

A team has to be correcting. That is what makes a team effective and two heads better than one. If you want to live alone and not be influenced by someone, then stay single. However, if you sign a marriage contract, it means you will have to allow yourself to be openly influenced by your helpmate. They are helping you change and grow those parts of yourselves that need adjusting. Often people say, "If you love me, then you shouldn't try to change me. You should accept me for who I am." I am challenging this thinking when it comes to marriage and relationships.

It is very important to allow our partner to help guide us towards improving our personal weaknesses. We cannot help but be influenced by certain qualities of the person we marry. We marry someone to uniquely be our "helpmate." This means that it is good to accept their help, including their prodding to diminish our weaknesses.

I understand that sometimes it's not the kind of help you were thinking you needed. I get it. For example, your husband thinks your marriage would benefit from a night without the children every couple of weeks. But you feel guilty about pulling yourself away from your two year old, because as you leave the house your toddler kicks, screams and possibly bites (I hope not, I may address tantrums in a future book). You don't think you need help from your helpmate, but your husband insists that you do. He complains that you are giving too much attention to your child and not enough to the marriage. He insists that the two of you need some time together and suggests that you leave your toddler with a babysitter. Your toddler is screaming when you leave the house, but after a couple of nights out on the town - chances are you will probably realize, for your own sanity, your partner was right.

It is important to recognize when your spouse's complaints are legitimate. By doing so, you are accepting the help you most likely need! If only you are humble enough to hear your partner's complaints and make adjustments accordingly, then you will become a more complete person and a better marriage helpmate. Additionally, if you find thoughtful ways to express your complaints to your partner and to ask them to make adjustments, your spouse can become a more complete person through marriage teamwork.

The bottom line of your marriage is this: if you service your spouse's complaints, you are more likely to have relationship, financial, and personal success.

I would like to give you examples of some positive outcomes from MarriageBiz. I recall meeting with a couple for therapy, and the husband ran a small, successful business. His wife focused her attention on their home and children. The husband admitted he was very happy in his marriage. His wife, on the other hand, was dissatisfied and was threatening to file for divorce if her husband did not make some adjustments.

During this first session, we clarified the two concerns she had. As she started to discuss her concerns, her husband became defensive and tried to explain the reasons for his behaviors. However, he was not proactively servicing and resolving his wife's complaints. The couple was stuck in a vicious cycle of the wife regularly complaining about the same problem, the husband becoming defensive, and the couple not reaching any resolution. In this case, I was easily able to ask the husband how he responded to complaints in his business. I then helped him respond the same way to his wife's complaints during the marriage counseling sessions via the MarriageBiz Steps outlined in Chapter 4. Within three sessions, this couple was finished with treatment and to my knowledge are doing very well.[28]

MarriageBiz concepts have also been a blessing to my own marriage. It has been both fun and helpful for my husband and I to discuss and work on the concepts of MarriageBiz together. Incorporating business ideas with our personal experiences (we hope to inspire and help other couples), has also served the purpose of better resolving our own differences! I can honestly say that sometimes when my husband and I are having a relationship disagreement, we remind each other the steps we are supposed to be taking to resolve

---

[28] Some couples may spend more than three sessions in marriage therapy if they have more concerns than the couple described in this example. Furthermore, the MarriageBiz approach is not meant for every couple. Rather, it is an approach that can be used to help couples who are struggling with conflict resolution. Some couples may be in treatment for other various issues, such as sex therapy for a problem in the sexual relationship, for addictions treatment, etc.

the problem – so we can get back to having fun. The business concepts in MarriageBiz help us better remember what the next step is in servicing our marriage complaints.

I am hopeful that MarriageBiz has changed some of your general attitudes about marriage service, how to make your complaints at the relationship service counter, how to service your spouse's complaints, and MarriageBiz strategies for an effective relationship service department.

I wish you great marriage success and profitability from following MarriageBiz principles! Specifically, I trust that MarriageBiz will become a constructive tool for servicing your marriage complaints. I urge you to be as ambitious about your marriage and home life as you are about your work and your financial life. The two aspects of your life are intricately intertwined, and I hope MarriageBiz helps symbolize just how much your work life and your personal life are tied together. As always, I am hopeful that you aim to be AmBizious for your family - putting your family first. Now, let's roll up our sleeves and get to work!

References

Curtis, John. (2006). The Business of Love: 9 Best Practices for Improving the Bottom Line of Your Relationship. IOD Press.

Gottman, J., Gottman, J. S., and & DeClaire, J. (2006). 10 Lessons to Transform Your Marriage. Three Rivers Press.

Inghilleri, L. & Solomon, M. (2010). Exceptional Service Exceptional Profit: The Secrets of Building a Five-Star Customer Service Organization. AMACOM Press.

Smith, D. (1998). Why Wives Complain More Than Husbands. USA TODAY (Society for the Advancement of Education).